ALDO PAVAN

the ganges

along sacred waters

With 267 illustrations, 253 in color

CONTENTS

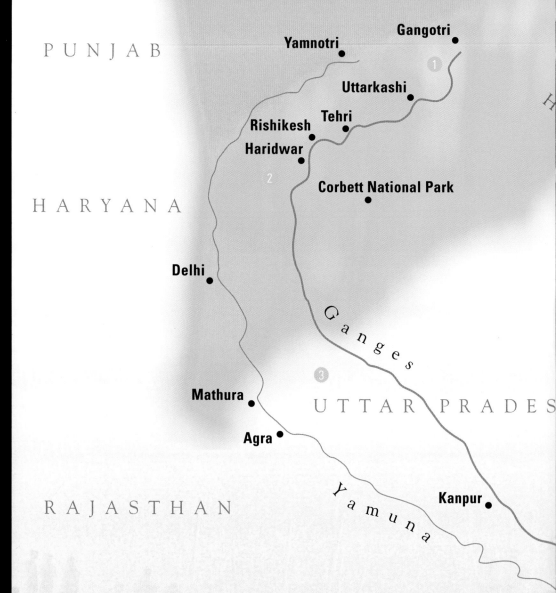

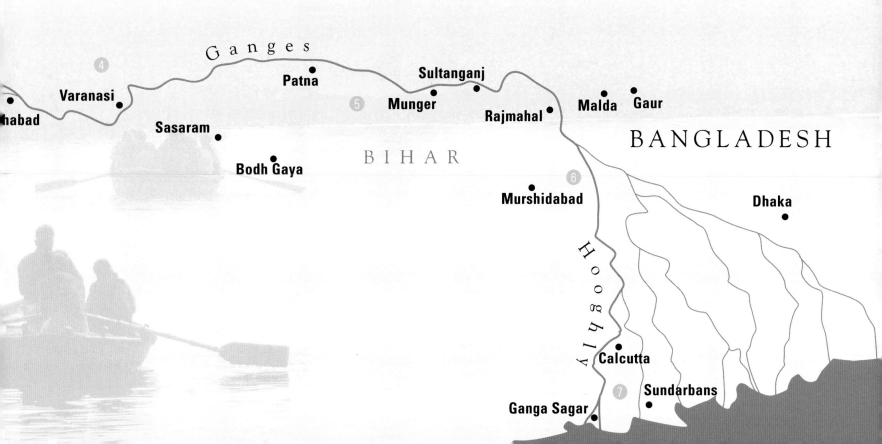

CHINA

TIBET

MALAYA

NEPAL

Kathmandu

BHUTAN

SIKKIM

Ganges

4

Varanasi

Patna

Sultanganj

Malda   Gaur

habad

5

Munger

Rajmahal

BANGLADESH

Sasaram

BIHAR

Bodh Gaya

6

Murshidabad

Dhaka

Hooghly

Calcutta

7

Sundarbans

Ganga Sagar

Page 1 The four brothers joyfully reunited – an episode from the *Ramayana*, an Indian epic poem.

Pages 2–3 Women on the banks of the Ganges at Rishikesh.

Pages 6–7 The ghats of Varanasi at dawn.

Pages 8–9 The garments of a *sadhu*, a holy man, hung out to dry at Allahabad on the Ganges.

Pages 10–11 Terraced fields in the high Ganges valley, near Uttarkashi.

Right The towering peak of Mount Shivling illuminated by the first rays of sunshine. The Gangotri glacier begins at the foot of this mountain; it is considered to be the principal life-giving source of the Ganges.

Opposite Ancient paintings that inspired the *Ramayana*, the epic tale inextricably linked with the Ganges.

ARUN HAD FINALLY REACHED THE GANGOTRI GLACIER. The very beginning. Here he has bathed in the waters flowing down from the Himalayas, and prayed to Mother Ganges, or *Ganga Ma* in Sanskrit. His whole life is a pilgrimage to attain holiness – naturally one made on foot. I ask him how long it would take to travel from the source to the mouth of the river. To travel the entire 2,500 kilometres that separate the mountains from the ocean? Arun smiles. He cannot answer with any certainty. 'Months, years,' he says, wearing a shirt far too thin for the degree of coldness here, at an altitude of over 4,000 metres. Surely he needs a jumper, or something warmer? 'No!' he exclaims. 'I don't need anything. When I am by the river I am like a child warming itself in its mother's arms.' Such is the sense of wonder cultivated among these third- millennium anchorites. A multitude in prayer, with a faith strong as iron. Alone, they stand before God, trying to liberate themselves from the cycle of death and rebirth.

The Ganges, the river sacred to half a billion Hindus, whose faith is the oldest known to man, is not merely a watercourse. It has neither the diversity nor the length of the Nile, nor the geological richness of the Congo, nor the history of the Tigris or the Euphrates. For Indians it possesses a much deeper significance: it is the river of all rivers, a river-god. It issues forth from the most majestic mountains on earth: it was Shiva who unleashed the power of Ganga, eldest daughter of Himavat, curbing her excessive force. The Ganges is the Mother Goddess, born of a divine act, and therefore a vessel that can carry prayer. In Vedic times the Ganges was already a sacred river, as were all the rivers in India. It only achieved pre-eminence later in the *Mahabharata*, where it was hailed as 'the ultimate place of pilgrimage', affirming that anyone who had bathed in it would thereby have purified seven descendants. The pilgrimage of the sadhu, or holy man, to the river source beyond the last temple on the Gangotri is purely symbolic. Like him, each year millions of pilgrims are drawn to all sections of the river in order to be blessed, to celebrate rituals, or simply to die and have their ashes scattered on the sacred waters.

The river gushes hurriedly down from the Himalayan gorges into the valley below. It flows impetuously through Rishikesh, home to many yoga schools and gurus, and then through Haridwar, the most holy city of the plain, the place where Vishnu left his footprint. The Gangetic Plain, which begins in Uttar Pradesh, is boundless. The divine waters of the Ganges are channelled to provide water for fields, and defiled by the out-

flows from factories and cities along its course. The river is the rice-bowl of a billion people. Half the population of India lives in the Ganges basin, which is the most densely populated area in the world. During the long summers, the monsoons shake the Ganges out of its usual stupor: the river bursts its banks and overflows, engulfing streets and countryside, claiming back its territory. The Indians are party to the rebellion of their deity.

At Allahabad the Ganges merges with the calm waters of the Yamuna, another river sacred to the Hindu religion, which almost runs dry at Delhi as it meets the needs of the city for water, but then flows onwards to lap the walls of the famous Taj Mahal and Agra Fort, both at Agra. Varanasi boasts of having been a city when Rome was still a collection of huts. With its monumental ghats, it is like a magnificent fresco depicting medieval India, both sorrowful and mystical. No city on the Ganges makes more of an impression. It enters into your bones and is unforgettable. Anyone who dies there is said to ascend directly into heaven. Scores of people go there to spend the last days of their life in the sweet anticipation of death – not a finality, but a transition into an intermediary stage.

When it reaches Bengal, the Ganges curves once again towards the south-east, dividing into numerous branches.

The biggest of these joins forces with the Brahmaputra 70 kilometres before Dhaka, forming a single course known as the Padma. This amalgamation of waters is as large as a sea. A hundred kilometres on in the valley, it empties into the Bay of Bengal, creating the Ganges-Brahmaputra Delta. It is a region of hurricanes and disastrous floods, a place where man has resigned himself to the forces of nature. But before encountering the Brahmaputra, the Ganges struggles to resist the call of the ocean by dividing into large rivulets. Hindus believe that the sacred course of the Ganges is the first one of these rivulets, the Hooghly, which bends decisively towards the south. It was here, on one of the thousands of fingers forming the river delta, that Calcutta (Kolkata) was born – a city encapsulating all the contradictions of the subcontinent. It epitomizes both the tragedy of the East and a concentration of evils imported from the West. Will Arun make it this far to gaze at the ocean? Perhaps, but for him it will not be the end of the road. In January, the pilgrims who have followed the course of the mystical river will embark on a boat bound for the temple of the goddess Ganga on the island of Sagar. It is the final act of purification they will make.

Opposite Another episode from the *Ramayana*. These drawings come from Chamba, an important centre of pahari painting situated in the Ravi valley, in the heart of the Himalayas.

Left Sunset over the dense forest that covers part of the islands in the Ganges Delta. Both humans and tigers inhabit this land of uncertain boundaries.

From the
Himalayan Glaciers

THE MORNING MIST SETTLES ON THE PINES AND DEODARS.

It hovers over the bottom of the valley through which the murmuring Ganges flows, still an unpre-possessing stream. The mist shifts silently, nudged along by the light breezes. It is magical, but also bone-penetratingly damp. The temperature is barely above freezing. Pilgrims climbing the slope with me are fleeting, shadowy ghosts whose footfalls scarcely make a sound. Some are shoeless, others wear simple sandals. All carry containers for the water of the holy river. Some are sadhus, holy men, but many are ordinary people, whole families, women, old folk and youngsters. There are overloaded mules and there are even litters, carried by four bearers. Many of my fellow travellers have left their villages for the first time in their lives especially to make this pilgrimage. It will take them many days, then they will return to their homes content. The waters will only be a memory. We are all wheezing up this pious path towards our goal, the glacier that gives life to India's holiest river, up there in the heart of the Himalayas. Bathers in this part of the river are guaranteed a clean body and a pure soul, their sins wiped away as if by a sponge. The holy ablution is cathartic.

Gangotri, 3,048 metres up in the mountains, is behind us. We still have about 23 kilometres to cover on foot. Step after step along the mule track, we continue breathless, our hearts pounding. The lack of oxygen is beginning to tell, but now the mist is rising. Slowly, my gaze takes in the valley for the first time. My eyes linger on bare slopes that have been polished by primordial moraine. Then in the distance, the dwelling of the gods reveals itself. The spectacular backdrop of the three peaks of Bhagirath, the white mountains of eternal snows, reaches a height of 6,680 metres. Opposite is the majestic, unclimbed, astonishing pinnacle of rock and snow known as Shivling, the 6,540-metre 'phallus of Shiva'. There is only a moment to rest your eyes on the sacred peaks of the Himalayas before the mist comes down again, and everything is as indistinct and empty as a dream. Imagination flies beyond these mountains to the pyramidal peak of Mount Kailash. According to Hindu mythology, this peak is Meru, the primordial mountain at the world's origin, and the beginning of life itself. A symbolic mountain, Meru is said to be the origin of the Ganges. Legend has it that the holy river rises from Lake Manasarowar, at the base of Meru, and runs through an underground tunnel to flow down the southern slopes of the Himalayas.

The flatlands lie about 300 kilometres further down. To get up there, you have to follow the course of the Ganges as it carves its way through the mountains in a series of ravines, gorges and waterfalls. You can reach Gangotri by car. The road is completely surfaced, but not without its dangers. You may be cut off by landslips caused by the summer rains, when water and mud submerge the blacktop. The village itself, which is inaccessible in winter, comes to life again from May to September. There are dozens of *ashrams*, or places of prayer, and *dharmashalas*, shelters for pilgrims, in Gangotri. Sadhus are everywhere. The main attraction is the temple dedicated to the holy river, or rather to the goddess called Ganga.

By now it is mid-morning. The sun has reappeared, and the air is getting thinner. The clouds chase each other across the sky like gamboling lambs. All at once, the broad Bhojbasa valley opens like an alpine pasture. We are 3,792 metres above sea level. The Himalayan peaks clasp the valley to their bosom. Beneath are meadows, above eternal snows. Here and there, red flags flutter wildly as if the wind is about to carry them off. They mark the Hindu hermits' shelters, makeshift tents or low huts made with stones from the Ganges. Some ascetics spend the whole winter praying and meditating, but my breath is getting shorter. My head feels heavy, and is starting to spin. Another 5 kilometres and I'll be there. Gaumukh, at 3,892 metres, is at the mouth of the Gangotri glacier, from which the Ganges flows. The waters hurtle down the mountain. Turbid and terrifying, they do not discourage bathers, washers, or those who have come to fill their containers with its holy liquid. Gaumukh, the 'cow's mouth', looks like a dark cave. The ice is grey, and dirty with deposits. Cracks and crumbling fissures can be seen. Huge sheets of ice fall away on to the riverbed. I look around in reverence and trepidation. Then I do what everyone else is doing. I take my shoes off and immerse my feet, at least, in the icy water.

A woman in a sari heads for the source. The summer sun has to battle with the clouds of the Bhagirathi valley. Rain is always imminent, and the ascent to the source of the Ganges becomes increasingly arduous. The higher you climb, the more you feel the lack of oxygen.

The water of the Ganges is so precious that it is never placed on the ground, even at night. This mustachioed pilgrim hails from far-off Rajasthan. He has travelled hundreds of kilometres to reach the source of the Ganges. In addition to the two containers we can see, he has a third hidden in his generous turban. The arrangement enables him to keep his balance as he walks. He is now heading back on foot to Rishikesh, about 300 kilometres further down the valley. It will take him several weeks, and he will sleep by the roadside, or in the dharmashalas, the shelters for wayfarers. He will cover the entire distance on foot. Walking is an important part of the pilgrimage, as it invites reflection and brings the walker closer to God. From the Indian capital, the pilgrim will catch a bus to his village. There, at last, he will be able to share out the holy water among his relatives and friends, who will keep it in their household shrine. According to popular belief, water from the source of the Ganges is miraculous because it stays pure for years.

Preceding pages
A sadhu, a holy man in red, preparing to bathe in the waters of the Bhagirathi, which looks torrential at this point. Washing is one way of cleansing negative *karma* accumulated in the past. Bathing in the Ganges guarantees a favourable rebirth. The source here is a *tirtha*, one of the most auspicious holy places of all, as are Allahabad and Varanasi. Traditionally, a tirtha is like a ford. It is a place of passage from the earth to Brahman, the kingdom of heaven.

Opposite Another sadhu on his way to the source of the Ganges. The trident he is holding is a symbol of Shiva. The god carried the river Ganges down from heaven on his matted hair after King Bhagiratha prayed for five thousand five hundred years beneath the Shivling to free the souls of the sixty thousand sons of King Sagara.

Right, top A young sadhu is carried on a litter to the source of the Ganges. His sanctity has earned him this privilege. He is said to be able to accomplish miracles, and is therefore treated with all due respect.

Right, bottom A very dangerous crossing on the Chirbasa, a tributary stream of the Ganges. It is in flood because a glacier upstream has unleashed a huge quantity of water, causing a sudden spate.

Preceding pages
The Gangotri glacier looks like a long grey tongue. About 28 kilometres long, the Gangotri descends from the 7,138-metre Mount Chaukhamba. To the right rise the three majestic peaks of Bhagirath, whose highest summit reaches 6,680 metres.

Opposite The solitary shadow of an ashram lengthens across the Bhojbasa plain, 3,792 metres above sea level. The source of the Ganges is at hand. The weather has worsened. Rain and mist loom. In winter, everything is buried under snow. Despite this, dozens of solitary, isolated sadhus live there. Red flags indicate the frugal residences of these Hindu hermits, some of whom even risk their lives by praying there throughout the terrible winter.

Below A shrine dedicated to Shiva.

Makeshift temples on the path to the source of the Ganges. Both feature the *lingam*, Shiva's phallus and the symbol of the god. To the right, the white bull Nandi, which Shiva rode upon to wage war on the demons. In many temples, the bull is placed in front of the main sanctuary to enable the god's faithful ally to keep watch over him. The coins are offerings left by pilgrims. These meagre funds are used by the sadhus to buy food.

The Ganges rises in the 28-kilometre-long Gangotri glacier, which descends from the slopes of Mount Chaukhamba. At least, that is the popular belief. In fact, the glacier's great, grey mass is washed and fed by the waters that pour down in summer from the peaks round about. You can see the Ganges in its liquid state again if you climb higher up to the glacial terrace of Tapovan, which extends beneath Shivling's towering peak.

We're off again. Bharat, the guide, shows the way. He knows how to negotiate the crevasses. Now we have to get round the front of the glacier, climb on to it, and then cross it before we tackle the final climb up to Tapovan, at 4,460 metres. The path is unmarked. The way ahead shifts with the movements of the glacier. Walkers have to avoid the cracks that can appear at any moment. Now, we seem to be going up into nothingness, to a sky where eagles are circling. The altitude makes me suffer. A gaggle of tanned Nepalese scurry downhill, bearing enormous loads of provisions and materials.

At last, the terrace of Tapovan comes into view, a huge, spectacular flower-filled expanse at the foot of Shivling. Nature provides the backdrop for a sacred setting. It was here that Bhagiratha prayed motionless for five thousand five hundred years, before the goddess Ganga bubbled forth from the sky to wash away the ashes of the sixty thousand sons of King Sagara. Here, the waters that descend from Shivling collect to form the Akash Ganga. Could this be the origin of the great river? Are these scattered, dribbling rivulets the great river Ganges? Bharat claims they are, and that this is the real source. 'There is no holier place a holy river could rise,' he explains.

Preceding pages
A temple made with stones taken from the bed of the Ganges, a few hundred metres from its source. This is the last opportunity for the Hindu faithful to pray as they walk to the origin of the sacred river.

Opposite A porter, weighed down, climbs towards the Bhagirath range of mountains.

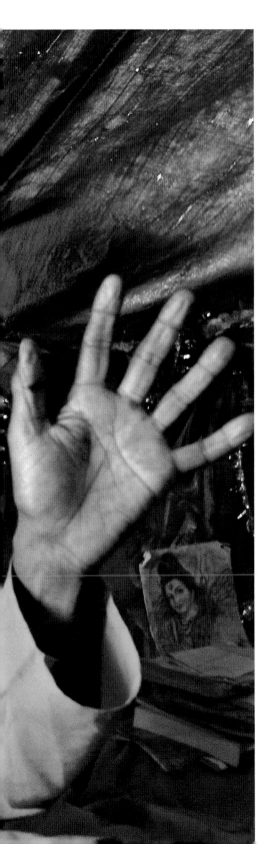

Preceding pages
The waters of the Ganges emerge from the mouth of the glacier at Gaumukh, at 3,892 metres above sea level. A sadhu meditates. Motionless on a rock, he defies the awful weather. He will stay there for hours, contemplating the waters that issue from the immense ice mountain.

Opposite A sadhu who lives in a tent made with scraps of material that he picked up on his way.

Right A pilgrim with containers to collect the water that gushes from the source.

Preceding pages
The Akash Ganga torrential
river rushes down from the
Shivling to flow through
the stunning Tapovan
valley, 4,460 metres above
sea level. Its waters feed
the Gangotri glacier, which
is why the Akash Ganga
is also considered sacred.
This remote spot is the
home of isolated sadhus
who have taken vows of
silence. Some have not
spoken for years. They
survive on the charity
of pilgrims.

Left A sadhu smoking
cannabis, which is widely
used in the Himalayas.

Opposite The village
of Gangotri nestles on
the banks of the Ganges
in a forest of deodars,
the Himalayan cedars.

Opposite A detail of the houses, which are entirely made of wood. The beams and doors are carved with motifs from an ancient iconography, inspired by the world of nature.

Right A snapshot of everyday life in the village of Harsil. In summer, the women sit outside to spin wool.

Preceding pages
A Brahmin officiates a religious rite on the banks of the river Ganges at Uttarkashi, a small town squeezed in among the mountains, 1,158 metres above sea level. A shell is used to raise the prayer to the sacred river. The rite is called *surya namaskar*. It is performed in the morning so that the day progresses satisfactorily. The shell is a reference to one of the attributes of the god Vishnu, the preserver of the universe, whose task it is to protect humankind.

Opposite A funeral pyre on the riverbank. The deceased's closest relative, perhaps a son, has just lit the fire that will consume the body. Other relatives look on. Once the wood has been burnt, the ashes are then sprinkled on the Ganges.

Right Members of the high-ranking Brahmin caste meet at the Hindu temple of Vishwanath in Uttarkashi for a ceremony. Their coloured garb is reminiscent of that worn once a year for *Makara Sankranti*, when the whole town takes part in a festive procession, bearing images of Hindu gods and goddesses.

Left A green-eyed, long-haired sadhu rests on the banks of the Ganges.

Opposite The sadhus' pilgrimage is a frugal one. They sleep and eat by the roadside, living on offerings from pilgrims. Sadhus lead a life of penitence and asceticism. Since they believe life on earth is an illusion, they reject earthly ties, and strive to free themselves from the negative cycle represented by karma. The saffron robes they wear signify that they have been washed symbolically in the fertile blood of Parvati, Shiva's consort. Contrary to common belief, some sadhus are women, like the one opposite, whom we surprised as she was resting on the road from Jahla to the village of Harsil. The three horizontal yellow lines on her forehead form the *tripundra*, the symbol of Shiva.

Preceding pages
A sadhu contemplates
the Ganges at Bhatwari.

Left On the road to the
source of the Ganges,
you meet hundreds of
sadhus, easily recognizable
by their red or orange
robes. Most travel alone
to observe the tradition
of silence and meditation.
Occasionally, the desire
to speak to someone leads
to impromptu gatherings,
especially when it is time
to light a fire and cook the
meagre meal. The ritual
pilgrim's pannikin holds
a small quantity of food,
which has to last the whole
day. Oddly enough, an
umbrella is one of the
few things that nearly
all sadhus carry.

Opposite A group
of pilgrims shelter from
the midday summer sun.

Overleaf A sadhu
continues on his way.

Preceding pages A series of terraced paddy-fields beside the river Ganges, between Tehri and Uttarkashi. Paddy-fields are a recurring theme in the long, spectacular valley carved out by the holy river. Cultivable areas alternate with ravines and waterfalls, and tiny villages look down from the sheer slopes.

Opposite A girl with a straw in her mouth, who has just climbed up to the village with a load of grass for the goats and hens.

Right A woman transplants shoots of rice.

Left A woman from one of the villages in the Ganges-Bhagirathi river valley stops at a pump to wash her pans.

Opposite A spectacular view of the paddy-fields beside the river Ganges.

Left, top Work in the paddy-fields involves both sexes. Whole villages take to the fields from morning to night. Here a woman repairs the bank of a rice terrace, while her husband leads oxen at the plough.

Left, bottom The field is flooded before ploughing to make it easier to work.

Opposite A series of terraces where the rice has just sprouted.

Overleaf A pilgrim makes his way round a wide curve in the Ganges near Tehri. In this part of the river, the countryside will be flooded by the new dam being built upstream to generate hydroelectric power. The scale of the project is gargantuan. The 260-metre-high dam will be the fifth largest in the world. When it is operational, around one hundred villages will be drowned. According to environmentalists, the new power station is at risk because it stands in an area that is prone to earthquakes. Between 1981 and 1991, the region suffered seventeen earthquakes. The authorities, however, refuse to listen to reason, and the bulldozers continue with their task. At some time in the future, this great sweep of the river will disappear forever.

The River Turns its
Back on the Mountains

Preceding pages
The evening ceremony
of *Ganga Aarti*, the
adoration of the river,
held on Haridwar's main
ghat, the Har ki Pairi.
The holy city stands at the
point where the Ganges
emerges from the last
foothills of the Himalayas.
The priests raise braziers
to the skies in prayer.

Opposite The morning
mist rises slowly over
the hills around the
village of Narendranagar,
1,173 metres up in the
mountains. After a few
kilometres of tortuous
descent through the thick
conifer woods, we come to
Rishikesh, where the vast
flatlands of the Ganges
plain seem very close.

HE CALLS IT GANGAJI. The 'ji' is the respectful form of address that Amistav uses to speak to the sacred river. For almost thirty years, he has lived on its banks and listened to the roaring current sending up clouds of rainbow-gleaming spray. 'You breathe a special energy here. Every particle is blessed,' he murmurs in rapture. 'The Ganges' water is rich in minerals. For centuries, the bodies of illustrious men have been burned on its banks. Their ashes have enriched the river with their positivity. For all these reasons, Gangaji is a concentrate of positive energy.' Amistav gave up his job as a civil servant. He exchanged a safe job for an uncertain future. Now, he lives off charity and walks, a pilgrim, along the holy roads. He sleeps in the ashrams, where he finds shelter, a plate of *dal*, the Indian lentil soup, and a little chapatti bread. He has no wife or children, and his family have long been forgotten. Now, his life is dedicated to sanctity. It is years since he set out on this path, and he would not turn back even today.

There are other sadhus like Amistav here in Rishikesh, the holy city that is renowned as India's most important centre for yoga. In the 1960s, Rishikesh gained international notoriety when the Beatles came to visit their guru. But long before it rose to world fame, Rishikesh was the refuge of wise men and intellectuals whose achievements became legendary. At 356 metres above sea level, it is the entrance to the sanctuary of the gods, the Himalayas. Four major Hindu pilgrimages leave from here for the sources of the rivers that form the Ganges: the Gangotri, Yamnotri, Kedarnath and Badarinath. These four locations have since time immemorial represented the most sacred of collective rituals. Rishikesh is where the door to heaven opens. The holy river, squeezed between steep, verdant cliffs, dominates the scene. One after the other, dozens of temples bow respectfully to the river. This succession of buildings has grown up, layer by layer, over the centuries since the day when, as popular belief would have it, Bharata, brother of the god Rama, stopped to meditate and do penance on this precise spot. Two audacious footbridges, called *jhoola*, meaning 'hammock-shaped', span the river. Called Lakshman and Shivanand, they are impressive, exciting and swarming with colourfully clad people. Each constitutes a leap towards the sacred huddle of ashrams, dharmashalas and riverside temples that stretch beneath the sheer cliffs of the Manikut Hills. It is almost an enclave, safe from the noise of motor rickshaws, car horns and spewing exhausts. It was here that, in the epic *Ramayana*, the god Hanuman picked the miracle-working herb Sanjivani to heal the mortal wounds of Lakshmana, the brother of Rama.

The sun has just come out. A rosy light rests on thick woods that appear as if by magic. Eyes need to be wide open. The nature park of Rajaji is nearby, and wild animals cross the road at this time of day. It is not unusual to find yourself facing a herd of elephants on their way to Corbett National Park. This time, we are out of luck, and have to make do with an apprehensive chital, a dappled axis deer, which shoots off into the undergrowth. After leaving Rishikesh, the Ganges turns its back on the mountains for good. It skirts the hills of Shivalik, the last offshoots of the Himalayas, now reduced to low, innocent-looking elevations. Finally at Haridwar, 320 metres above sea level, the great river settles down. The impetuous young girl has now grown up, and is ready to begin the journey that will take her across the vast flatness of the Gangetic Plain. Haridwar means 'gateway of the gods'. One of the steps of the main ghat, or landing, known as ghat Har ki Pairi (the 'descent of god') bears the footprint of the god Vishnu. Every twelve years, the *Kumbhamela* is held there. This great ritual attracts millions from all over India.

We arrive in Haridwar just after dawn, and the pilgrims are already beginning their ritual immersion in the sacred river. They hold on to heavy iron chains, or each other, so as not to be swept away by the current. Meanwhile, other pilgrims are swarming over the banks that at night host their impromptu camps. Vendors and beggars are already at work. A hairdresser has set up shop on one of the bridges, and is now combing a wig that will serve as a model. A little further on, a snake-charmer extracts his cobra from a wicker basket. A young *chela*, or disciple, begs for offerings for his master, a sadhu who has vowed not to speak for four years. He waits in the shade as the sun begins to beat down. Sacred and profane mingle as sunset – the day's most important moment – approaches. This is when the ceremony of *Ganga Aarti* is celebrated. This liturgy in honour of Mother Ganges involves floating baskets of offerings on the river with a lamp burning in them. At sunset, the real world steps aside for magic.

Three kilometres north of Rishikesh is the 240-metre-long Lakshman Jhoola footbridge over the Ganges. Until 1889, there was a rope bridge there, and this chain bridge dates from 1939. Thousands of pilgrims pour on to the left bank of the great river. They are heading for the Kailashanand Mission Ashram, dedicated to Shiva and run by the Kailashanand Mission Trust. Rishikesh is India's main yoga centre, and the town is thick with ashrams. Legend has it that this is where the door of the god's throne of heaven, the Himalayas, is located. Bharata, brother of the god Rama, is said to have stopped there on the advice of the wise Vasishtha to do penance for killing Ravana, king of Lanka. In the heart of this chaotic town, near the main ghat, Triveni, is the temple dedicated to the legendary Bharata. The Ganges at this point flows between sheer walls of vegetation-clad mountains that rise up like giants.

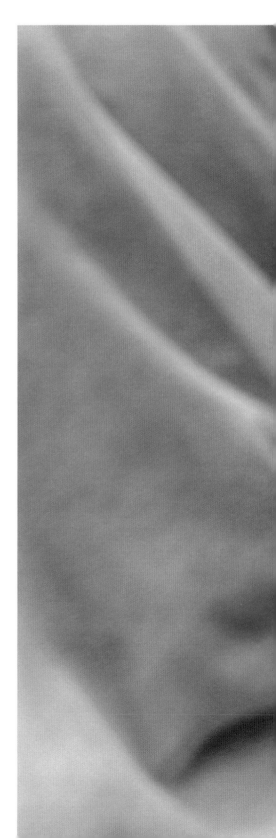

Left and opposite
Another bridge, Shivanand Jhoola, spans the Ganges just outside the centre of Rishikesh, linking the ashrams of Shivanand and Swarg. The ambitious, recently built structure proved necessary to deal with the large numbers of pilgrims. As well as the bridge, there are also ferries to link the two banks.

Overleaf Another view of the Shivanand Jhoola. In the background is the left bank of the Ganges, where the Swarg ashram is situated.

Preceding pages
A Sikh pauses to observe the Ganges from the Lakshman Jhoola bridge. According to legend, this is the exact spot where Lakshmana, Rama's brother, crossed the sacred river on jute ropes to meditate on the other side. The incident is related in the *Ramayana*, the sacred text that tells the epic exploits of the god Rama. On the right bank of the Ganges is a much-frequented temple dedicated to Lakshmana.

Left The entrance to one of the temples of the Kailashanand Mission Trust, founded in 1954 by one of the most celebrated gurus in the recent history of Rishikesh, His Holiness Swami Jee Maharaj. In addition to founding a school of yoga and meditation, the swami is also involved with natural medicine and the *Ayurveda*. His charitable initiatives include a shelter for those afflicted by Hansen's disease (leprosy). The structure in this photograph is called the Kailashanand Mission Ashram, like the one on the left bank of the Ganges. Both stand solemn and imposing, concealing a maze of stairs and passageways that lead from one floor to the next.

Opposite A sadhu at the door of the temple.

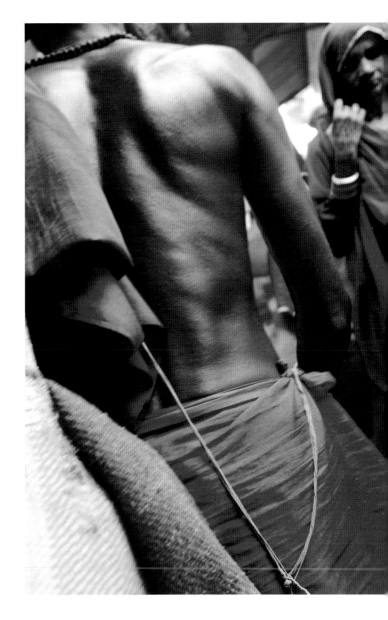

Opposite A group of women prepare to bathe in the Ganges at the ghat beneath the Shivanand Jhoola in Rishikesh.

Right The bronzed chest of a Brahmin, recognizable by the cord hanging from his shoulders. A steep flight of steps leads from the temple of Lakshmana to the road along the right bank of the Ganges. When the crowds are at their thickest, it can be difficult to get through.

Preceding pages
A group of women in
brightly coloured saris
sit near the temple in
Rishikesh dedicated to
Lakshmana. They are
resting before heading
towards the dharmashala,
the shelter for pilgrims,
where they will spend the
night. In June and in the
summer months, when
Rishikesh is at its busiest,
devotees flood in from all
over India. The city seems
to be bursting at the seams
with all these visitors.

Left A small temple to
Shiva stands on the left
bank of the Ganges near
the Shivanand Jhoola.
It is the monsoon season.
Rain looms. The clouds
are darkening, and the
humidity is so high that
it is difficult to breathe.

Opposite Shiva's trident
defies the late afternoon
humidity, which has
turned into a thick,
straw-coloured mist.

Opposite A priest is colouring the statue of the popular monkey god, Hanuman.

Right A woman prepares the offerings that will be used in the evening for the adoration of the Ganges. Baskets containing the offerings and a small lamp are placed in the water by the faithful, as an act of prayer to the sacred river.

For the past two hours, we have been following the broad bed of the river Ramganga. Inquisitive monkeys examine us in silence. Sleepy crocodiles stretch motionless in the sun. A few sambars, large Indian deer, skip briskly away when the bulky frame of the elephant we are riding crashes noisily through the undergrowth. The howdah we are sitting in bounces about as we proceed along the rock-strewn path. Then, at last, there it is! I think I can see the yellow and black stripes. It is our third day of searching, but at last our persistence has paid off. Before us stand not one but two tigers, hiding behind a low bush. One lazy-looking beast is lying down, but the other stares at us, ready to pounce. Our elephant goes closer. My breath quickens, and a primeval fear clutches my throat. The elephant takes one step, then another. We are eye to eye with the tigers. Then our mount decides it has had enough. The big cats bore it, so it raises its trunk and trumpets a warning. The two tigers shake themselves, then spring to their feet. They roar and regally depart, without hurry and in all solemnity. In the meantime, I have gone pale. The roar froze my blood. It sounded to me like an awful, gut-wrenching cry of despair.

The Corbett National Park, covering an area of some 1,134 square kilometres in the foothills of the Himalayas, is the tigers' domain. It is home to ninety-three examples of an animal that has been hunted for centuries by humankind, and is now under threat of extinction. Luckily, Project Tiger, launched in 1973, has encouraged an increase in the numbers of these big cats. The battle still has a long way to go. In addition to poachers, tigers have to face another, even worse enemy – the growing population. Human settlements are eating up the last remnants of wild India – the India that Mowgli, Rudyard Kipling's jungle boy, once knew.

A tiger lurks in the vegetation of the Corbett National Park, named after the great English hunter. Jim Corbett's efforts to defend villages plagued by man-eating tigers made him a legend. In the late nineteenth century, tigers that had acquired a taste for human flesh were a significant danger. In some cases, a single tiger might devour hundreds of people before it was killed. Corbett put his unerring aim at the disposal of the authorities, facing the man-eaters with incredible courage.

Opposite An elephant transports a group through the Corbett park savannah. If they are lucky, they may catch a glimpse of one or two tigers. Today, this vast area at the foot of the Himalayas has been declared a nature park and named after Jim Corbett. It is part of the official Indian project to protect the tiger.

Right A group of elephants being washed at the end of the working day. The operation is performed by rubbing down their skin with large flat stones taken from the river.

Preceding pages
An elephant crosses the
Ramganga at dawn. The
river is the source of life in
the vast wilderness of the
Corbett National Park.

Left An old photograph
of a tiger hunt, showing
British hunters as well
as Indian aristocrats.

Opposite A young artist
paints a surrealist portrait
of a tiger. The big cat is one
of the symbols of India in
popular culture.

Overleaf The Ganges
in flood. Here, the river
flows through the holy
city of Haridwar on a
very warm late summer's
afternoon. From this point
on, the Ganges crosses
the flatlands, leaving the
mountains behind.

Preceding pages
The climax of the evening
Ganga Aarti ceremony.
The crowd swarms over
the Har ki Pairi, Haridwar's
most important ghat.
Repetitive singsong fills
the air as the pilgrims
put their lit lamps on the
water to be borne away
on the river.

Opposite A woman who
has come to the holy city
of Haridwar to pray. She
has travelled on a bus with
the rest of her family and
is carrying a small bundle
on her head, possibly
containing a change of
clothes and some food.

Right A snake charmer
and his cobra perform for
money, taking advantage
of the hordes of pilgrims
who have come to
Haridwar to pray.

Left A beggar takes a break on the right bank of the Ganges at Haridwar.

Opposite Some young people dive into the Ganges to escape the heat that grips Haridwar in the period prior to the July monsoons.

Overleaf Another group of women on a pilgrimage to Haridwar. The bank of the Ganges provides somewhere to rest or sleep between prayers.

Left The stop for motor
rickshaws, the most
economical means
of public transport.
A young woman has
the palm of her hand
decorated with henna,
an ancient beauty
treatment whose origins
are lost in the mists
of time.

Opposite The red turban
of a farmer who has arrived
in Haridwar from distant
Gujarat after spending
several days on buses.
The pilgrimage to the
Ganges has to be made
at least once in a person's
lifetime, even if it is
arduous and expensive.

Opposite A mother in Haridwar bathes her child in the holy waters of the Ganges. The little boy has just had his head shaved as a token of purification.

Right Three women take it in turns to bathe, holding each other's hands so as not to be carried off by the strong current.

Overleaf A group of young people jump into the river for a swim. They have been praying under the guidance of their guru, and have shaved their heads as a sign of renewal and devotion.

Opposite An ancient, semi-abandoned home in Haridwar.

Right A truck transports a group of pilgrims dressed as sadhus. Their temple supervisor probably organized this trip to pray in the holy cities of the upper Ganges.

Encounter with the
Vast Plain

THE PLAIN, FLAT AND INFINITE, AND THE CROWD. Here, the Himalayas seem like a white and pure dream, a memory so poignant it makes you ache with longing. The feelings experienced up among those summits melt away like ice, leaving behind them morainic detritus: pure air, silence, humility and hard work, symbolized by the small plots of land for the cultivation of rice. The wry smiles of the people up there, condemned to live a life in which a few daily essentials must suffice. The labour of the ploughman, ankle-deep in mud. The women's hands submerged in water, transplanting rice seedlings. Panniers laden with wood. Here on the plain it is a different story. The hard work is the same, but multiplied by infinity: cars, rickshaws, noise, horns blaring, cows, coloured saris. People. Hordes and hordes of people. And in summer, as it is now, add to that the heat, also to the nth degree. Unrelenting heat. Forty degrees is the norm. The monsoon is just around the corner, heralding the onset of the rains so welcomed for crop cultivation. But it also threatens destruction, with the banks of the Ganges swollen to bursting point and the fear of flooding in Bengal, waters overflowing, houses swept away, livestock drowned, and death lying in ambush. Blessing and tragedy. A natural cycle, but an overwhelming one, which man will fail to conquer, however hard he tries.

This is the India of the third millennium – around one billion inhabitants, and the population is destined to increase still further, with a perverse taste for large numbers. Where do we go from here? Will there be enough space for everyone? How many more mouths can be fed? Constant beeps on the horn, skids and sharp brakes as we journey to Delhi. The driver negotiates head-on collisions and questions. The bare feet of the imperturbable sadhus tracing the path to the sources of the Ganges are a reminder that nothing changes over the centuries. Perhaps all is immanence. That buffalo spurred to a gallop by his owner – what does he know of modernity? The cart harnessed to the powerful beast is laden with sugar cane. Increase in GDP? India as a developing country? Toyotas with air-conditioning are whizzing past. Two worlds are touching but not communicating; they are trying only to avoid each other and not to collide with each other. No record is kept of all the accidents along the road – mere hazards of life. The demographic explosion, the chaos, the struggle of daily life are both apparent and illusory. India prays, kneeling on the banks of the Ganges, suffering as it did a century ago, as it did in the dim and distant past.

'Nothing of substance changes,' Rajeev tells me as he emerges from the Yamuna. 'This has always been the most sacred of all the rivers in India, and it always will be. The god Krishna played here as a child. Surely this is enough?' 'What about the Ganges?' I ask him. 'That is also sacred,' he answers, 'but don't the scriptures say that one dip in the Yamuna is worth one hundred in the Ganges?' The Yamuna river is about 1,370 kilometres long, and has its source in the Himalayas, like the Ganges. Its course flows down to Delhi and then on towards Agra, passing Vrindavan and Mathura, considered to be sacred cities because Krishna spent his youth in them. The Yamuna merges with the Ganges at the gates of the city of Allahabad (confusingly also known as Prayag), at the point where the mythical subterranean river Sarasvati, quoted in the *Veda*, is also said to join them. Everyone prays to his own god, Krishna of the Yamuna or Shiva of the Ganges. The important thing is to live a holy life, or at least to try to do so.

Rajeev is a civil servant, one of nearly two million inhabitants at Agra. Each morning he comes here to wash. The early morning had been humid and dismal, with a weak sun struggling to break through the uncertain clouds. Now there is a veil of yellow mist hanging in the air, making it hard to breathe. The silhouette of the Taj Mahal is outlined ahead, the monumental tomb built by a heartbroken king in honour of his wife. Magnificence and splendour; echoes of the ostentation of Islam on Indian soil. Down below flows the Yamuna, a sad and emaciated Yamuna, a rivulet lost in an enormous bed. A child lost in the vast riverbed of the world. There is very little water. Almost all of it is used up at Delhi, to quench the thirst of the ten million inhabitants there. It does not even resemble the powerful river it once was. 'It is said to be polluted, and that not even a fish can survive in it, but when I raise my cupped hands full of water to the sky, I can smell the heady perfume of sandalwood it releases…' Rajeev enthuses. 'Isn't that a sign that appearances can be deceptive? That this is indeed a sacred river?' Confronted with faith, there are no explanations.

A flower carved in marble, a detail of the wall decorations in the Taj Mahal.

Preceding pages
A sea of columns at the
Qutb Minar complex at
the gates of Delhi. The
city is on the Yamuna,
a tributary of the Ganges,
considered to be sacred
because the god Krishna
grew up on its banks.
Bathing in the Yamuna
is a form of purification.

Left A woman
showing her hands
painted with henna.

Opposite A group
of women visit the Qutb
Minar complex in Delhi.

Left Detail of ornaments worn by a young bride visiting the sumptuous mausoleum of the emperor Akbar, built in red sandstone. Akbar was one of the most important Islamic rulers of India under the Moghul dynasty. The funerary monument is at Sikandra, 4 kilometres north-west of Agra, in the midst of lush green gardens where dozens of deer graze in the wild. The structure is a blend of various architectural styles borrowed from Hinduism, Jainism, Western Christianity and, of course, Islam. Construction was begun by Akbar himself as an almost tangible proof that the fusion of different schools of thought was possible, a hypothesis to which the emperor adhered strongly, creating a syncretic school of philosophy based on monotheism and religious tolerance.

Opposite A group of women file past the decoration on the central building, which houses the tomb of Akbar.

Preceding pages
Detail of the exquisite marble tracery on sandstone on the mausoleum of Akbar. The emperor was one of the most illustrious rulers of the Moghul dynasty. In addition to his considerable military prestige, conquering parts of Afghanistan, Bengal, Kashmir and the Deccan, he also showed great statesmanship in his efforts to mediate between the Islamic world and the Hindu world, leading to a peaceful coexistence between the two peoples. Although he achieved notable results during his reign, the momentum was lost after his death at Agra in 1605.

Opposite and right
A symphony of geometric shapes form the marble decorations on the mausoleum of Akbar.

Overleaf
The mausoleum's imposing entrance is red sandstone studded with white marble.

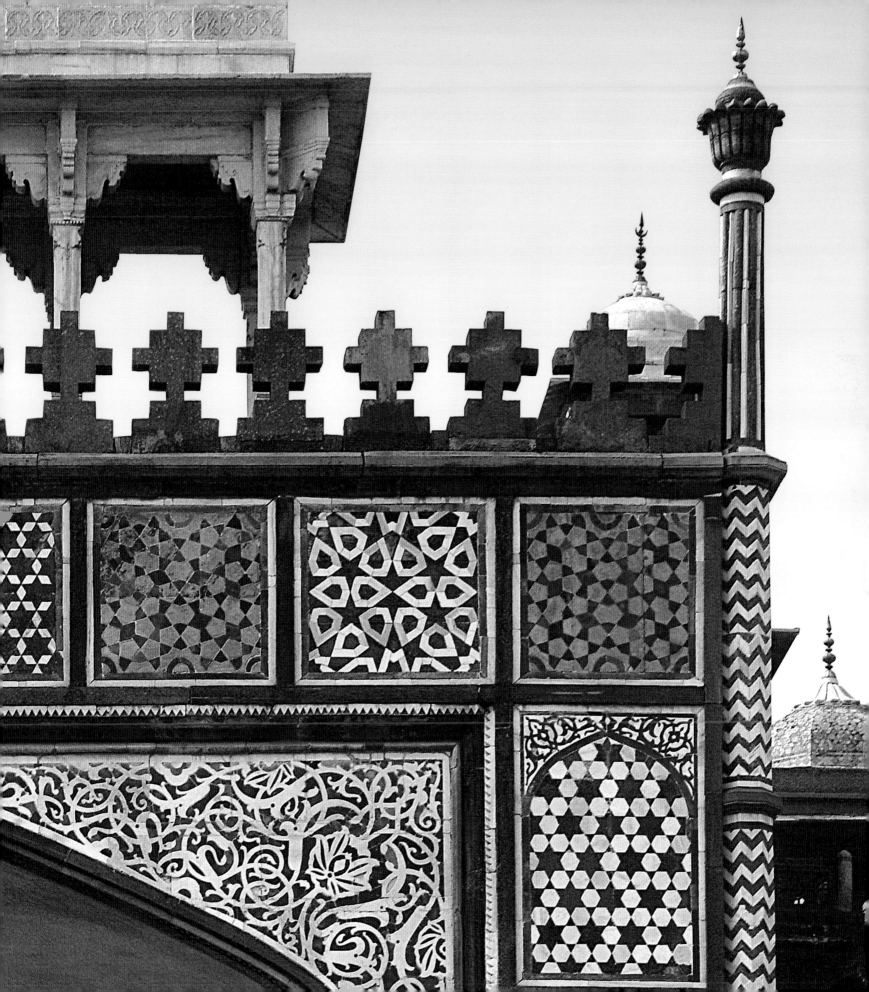

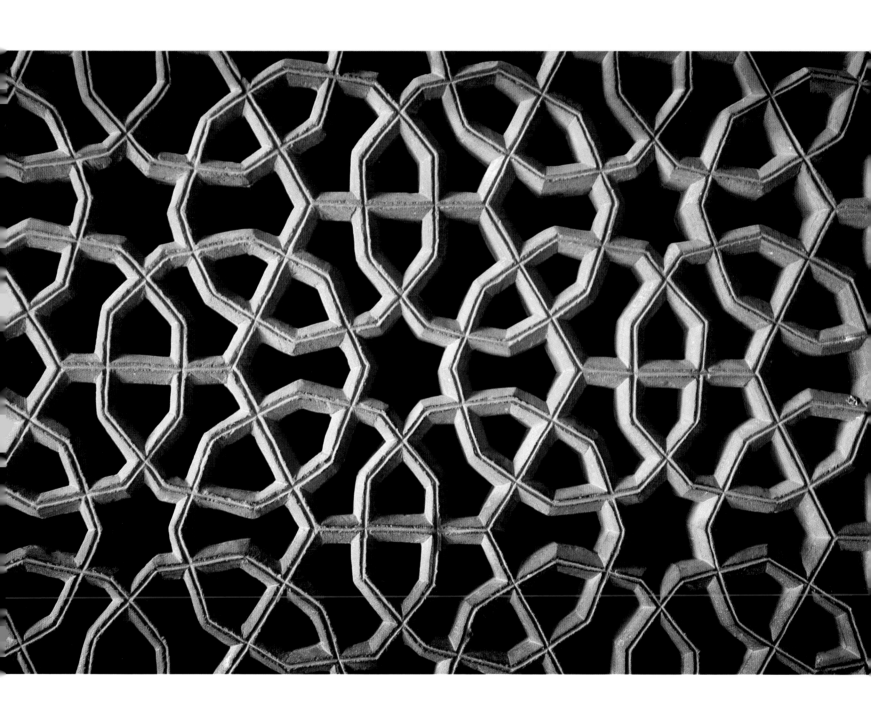

Opposite View of the Diwan-i-Am, the public reception room inside the Agra Fort, built by Shah Jahan to receive dignitaries and the numerous petitioners.

Right An exquisite detail of the Diwan-i-Am. In an unusual exception to the Islamic rule that forbade representation in art, a flowering plant is portrayed by delicately inlaid coloured marble.

Overleaf
The magnificent palace of Itimad-ud-Daulah, known as the 'Little Taj-Mahal', reflected in the waters of the Yamuna river at sunset. This tributary of the Ganges is also believed to be sacred. According to Hindu tradition, the god Krishna, the incarnation of Vishnu, grew up in the nearby city of Mathura and bathed in the waters of the river as a young boy. The warm glow of the last rays of sunshine caresses the delicate lace-like trelliswork of marble and semi-precious stones. Pre-dating the Taj Mahal, it was built between 1622 and 1628 as the tomb of Mirza Ghiyas Beg, Moghul prime minister.

Opposite Mother and son step over the marble trellis threshold of the inner sanctuary in the Taj Mahal, which houses the remains of Mumtaz Mahal, the beautiful second wife of Shah Jahan. She died in childbirth in 1631. Distraught over the tragedy, her husband decided to build a magnificent mausoleum as an everlasting memorial to his great love for her. Construction began in the year of her death and involved twenty thousand workers. It took twenty years to complete. It is still not known who designed the building, but it is thought to be the fruit of a team that included the architect Isa Khan, of Iranian origin, and a number of other craftsmen seemingly from Europe, and Venice in particular.

Right The Taj Mahal seen from the imitation mosque on the eastern side of the palace.

Overleaf Detail of marble mosaics in the mausoleum. The most precious decorations were executed using a technique called *pietra dura*, involving the insertion of semi-precious stones into the marble. In the morning the Taj Mahal is a pinkish yellow colour, and milky white in the evening. It turns golden when the moon shines on it.

Preceding pages
The Taj Mahal and, on
the left, the Yamuna river,
whose water level dropped
dramatically following
the construction of a series
of barriers designed to
guarantee the provision
of adequate water for
Delhi and for the irrigation
of fields.

Opposite A Muslim
woman visits the tomb
of Sheikh Salim Chishti,
whom the emperor Akbar
visited over five hundred
years ago in order to
ask that he might be
blessed with a male child.
Ever since then, infertile
women have gone there
to pray. His tomb is in the
Jama Masjid mosque in
Fatehpur Sikri, the fortified
city that was the capital
of the Moghul Empire
between 1571 and 1585
before being abandoned.
According to legend,
the city was built by
Akbar after he received
a prophecy from Sheikh
Salim Chishti, which
predicted that he would
have three sons. The
emperor was so impressed
by the clairvoyance of the
holy man that he decided
to turn the insignificant
little village of Fatehpur
Sikri into the capital of his
empire. Unfortunately the
city was abandoned after
only fourteen years,
perhaps due to a lack of
water. Akbar relocated his
residency to Lahore, and
the abandoned Fatehpur
Sikri fell into neglect as fast
as it had grown up. Since
then nothing has changed.
Today it is a splendid
example of Moghul
architecture, unrivalled
throughout India.

Right Detail of a
pomegranate carved in
red sandstone.

Overleaf
A decorative detail.

Preceding pages
View of the ornamental
pool in Fatehpur Sikri,
adjacent to the private
audience chamber
of Akbar.

Opposite Two Muslim
women dressed in black
cross the courtyard of the
Jama Masjid mosque in
Fatehpur Sikri. They have
come from nearby villages
in order to pray.

Right A group of young
Hindu women with their
brothers visiting Fatehpur
Sikri. For them too this
museum-city provides
a way to explore India's
Islamic past.

Overleaf The monumental
gateway of the Jama
Masjid mosque, called
Buland Darwaza, or the
Gate of Victory. It was built
to commemorate Akbar's
conquest of Gujarat.

naifs painted
backs of
Allahabad.

This time we took the train, the 'night train', in order to avoid the scorching road between Agra and Allahabad. A six-hour journey with air-conditioning. At the station a sign says 'No spitting'. We will try to heed the warning, but we do not chew the nuggets of betel, the reason for the red stains blotted all over India from the north to the south. In the waiting room, the blades of the fan seem tired, as if they have been rotating for a thousand years in vain. Coolness is a mere theoretical concept. But occasionally there is just enough of it to bring a short respite to tired limbs. Not only do we have to share our surroundings with a large mouse, which is hiding behind our wooden seats, but it also disturbs us with its continual squeaking. From the couchette, night is visible in all its splendour.

It is five in the morning when we arrive in Allahabad, and the city is shaking itself from sleep. There is already a trickle of people heading for Sangam, the precise point where the waters of the Yamuna merge with those of the Ganges. This is considered to be one of the most sacred parts of the river, where past and future sins can be washed away. This is why once every twelve years Allahabad plays host to the *Kumbhamela* (also known as the *Kumbh Mela*, or 'pot festival'), a religious festival that attracts people from all over India and is deemed to be one of the most spectacular gatherings in the world. For about eight weeks between ten and twenty million pilgrims converge here. Astrologists calculate the most auspicious days for the ablutions, and draw up a kind of schedule for taking sacred baths. The cities of Haridwar, Ujjain and Nasik also take turns in hosting the festival, although the one held in Allahabad is the most imposing. This event is called Maha, which means 'big', and takes place in January or February, when the sun enters Aries and Jupiter is in Aquarius.

An image captured at dawn in Allahabad. At first light, people set out along the banks of the Ganges on foot or by bicycle, heading for Sangam, the precise point where the great river merges with the waters of the Yamuna. This confluence is considered to be the most important part of the entire course of the Ganges. It is also supposedly the point where it is joined by the mythological and invisible river Sarasvati, mentioned in the sacred scriptures of the *Veda*. The *Kumbhamela* takes place there every twelve years.

Left A sadhu approaches the precise confluence of the Ganges with the Yamuna, blowing into a shell as a sign of prayer.

Opposite A haircut on the banks of the Ganges.

Overleaf Boats at dawn in Sangam.

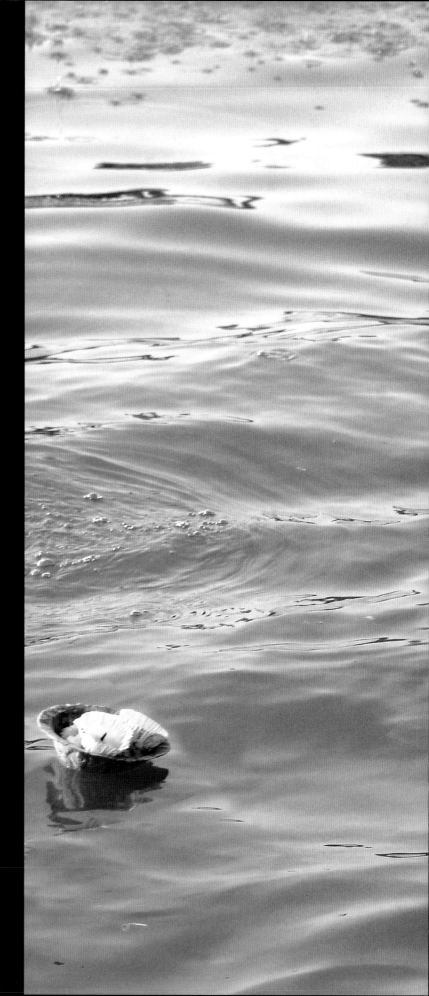

The Sacred Waters
of Varanasi

Preceding pages
A woman immerses
herself in the Ganges
at Varanasi in an act
of purification, reciting
a personal puja, or prayer.
The small baskets with
candles are an offering
to the gods.

Opposite A thousand-
year-old ritual performed
on the ghat at Varanasi:
a priest celebrates a daily
rite to the rising sun by
repeatedly lifting a brazier
up to the sky. The flames
have a significance
because they are a symbol
of purification. While this
ritual – known as *aarti* – is
taking place, the sky itself
is changing into a myriad
of colours, from pink, to
violet, to blue. The city
of Varanasi has its roots
deeply embedded in
previous centuries. Since
the first millennium BC
it has been a centre of
philosophy, religion
and Indian science.

NIGHT ENVELOPS THE BANKS OF THE GANGES. It shrouds people and objects in uncertainty and inky blackness. Silhouettes appear – perhaps ectoplasms from another world perforating the real world. Even the river water is like pitch. On the ghat, the few lights are struggling against obscurity, as if lacking the oxygen necessary to burn. A boatman approaches the riverbank, followed by another. They are whispering to a Brahmin who wears the thread of life slung across his bare chest. An indistinct splash in the water. Could it be a body? Sombre shapes are visible amidst the flotsam and jetsam. Perhaps they are men. Nearby, oxen or some other animals are crouching down – possibly a tangle of monkeys. I can make out the face of Hanuman, the monkey-god, baring his teeth at me, but it is only a bas-relief painted in red. Suddenly a hole is torn in the thick black veil of night, revealing a group of figures bearing a stretcher covered in an orange shroud. They are accompanied by bells and tambourines. The wrapped corpse is being borne swiftly to the Manikarnika ghat. Hell lurks around the corner. Further on, there are huge piles of firewood, the logs for the funeral pyres that the Doms, the untouchables, will shortly be weighing in order to establish the price of the deceased with the family. Then darkness prevails and the tear in the veil is sewn up again. Everything is black once more, appallingly black. Appalling in its intensity as it waits to be liberated by the new dawn, by the daylight that will cleanse the air, wipe out the shadows and banish fear. This city has the power to cause sickness and destruction, and to wound the spirit. Surely it must be sacred to Shiva, the ambivalent god, Destroyer and Creator?

My thoughts whirl dizzily in painful turmoil as my legs carry me towards this hell, this ghat that has engulfed the orange stretcher. Still dawn has not broken. I hope that my watch has not stopped, and then finally across the river a faint light announces the new day, the liberator. A swarm of untouchables approach me. For a fistful of rupees they will conduct me to Hades. They have distinctive faces with over-sized eyes, or so it seems to me. Untouchable but indispensable, for sooner or later they are needed by everyone to ensure safe passage into the afterlife. Anyone not living in Varanasi is taken there to die, for that way paradise can be guaranteed – an escape from the cycle of *samsara*, of reincarnation. The rich are obliged to spend their last years there; for them death is a luxury that can be purchased. That is why the untouchables have become powerful, even insolent. One of them takes charge of me and we set off. We head for the place dedicated to the disposal of the body, the outer shell that houses the spirit, and whose ashes will be scattered in the river. The stench in the air hits you in the stomach – acrid and bitter. Two, three, four pyres almost burnt out, with only embers remaining. The orange stretchers have been tossed on to the ground. They await their turn in a queue, ordered and splendid; the sole things of beauty in this abyss. Look, there is a man walking round a freshly built pyre. He circles it three times, then sets it alight. Maybe he is the son of the deceased. He certainly should be according to the saying that people in India want to have sons in order to ensure themselves a proper funeral. A final blaze of glory. A red glow spreads across the ghat; the faces of the relatives seem to echo a pitiless lament…and everywhere the insistent, giant-eyed gaze of the servants of death. One of them blocks my way. He wants money – more rupees, more rupees. The European has witnessed the destruction, he has descended into hell and now he must pay. His voice seems to come from the stomach, distant and disembodied. Maybe it is coming from the afterlife.

Shiva may be the Destroyer, but he is also the giver of new life. I retrace my steps. The morning light over Varanasi has redeemed life, and all is resurrected. But the nightmares have not yet gone; they are lengthening like disturbing shadows. As the sun rises on the horizon and the city stretched along the left bank of the Ganges is caressed by its golden rays, a priest lifts his voice in praise of the new day. It is a thousand-year-old rite that has been lost in the mists of time. His arms raise a flaming brazier repeatedly up to the sky, which is now clearing, blue giving way to violet. Shiva is now the Creator. The beggars get up from their stone pallets under the walls of palaces built by the rich and by the maharaja. The sadhus take their places at the river and begin their ceremonial bathing. They pray and bathe in the same water in which the ashes of the dead are floating, and not infrequently the bloated carcasses of animals, or the unburnt remains of human corpses that have fallen into the river. The crowd is thronging on the steps again.

Opposite Another scene typically found on the ghats of Varanasi: an Aghora sadhu has smeared himself with ashes and is bringing his body into submission by means of a contortionist posture. This is an ascetic practice designed to punish oneself for approaching god.

Overleaf View of the ghats of Varanasi and the Ganges touched by the first rays of sunlight. These temples and buildings are next to the Scindia ghat. The most popular ghat is Dasaswamedh. According to tradition, this is the place where Brahma put King Divodasa to the test, sacrificing ten horses. Since then, the Dasaswamedh ghat has become of the most famous tirtha in India, and therefore a holy place to bathe.

Left, above A priest prepares a funeral rite.

Left, below A corpse wrapped in an orange sheet awaits incineration on a funeral pyre. For Hindus, fire represents the means by which the soul is transported to the next life. Varanasi is the most propitious city in which to die and be cremated. The bodies are looked after by people from the lowest caste, known as Doms. For centuries they have been the guardians of the sacred fires for cremation. Each year thousands of corpses pass through their hands, perhaps forty or fifty thousand. Funerals are expensive, especially if they involve special funerary rites, and the Doms have no scruples about increasing the prices in order to extort as much money as possible. Their thirst for money is proverbial. Electric cremation costs less and is being encouraged by the authorities.

Opposite A group of people, probably relatives about to participate in a funeral, soap themselves before performing their ablutions. Similar scenes are to be found all along the ghats where cremations take place. The most important of these is the Manikarnika ghat, one of the oldest.

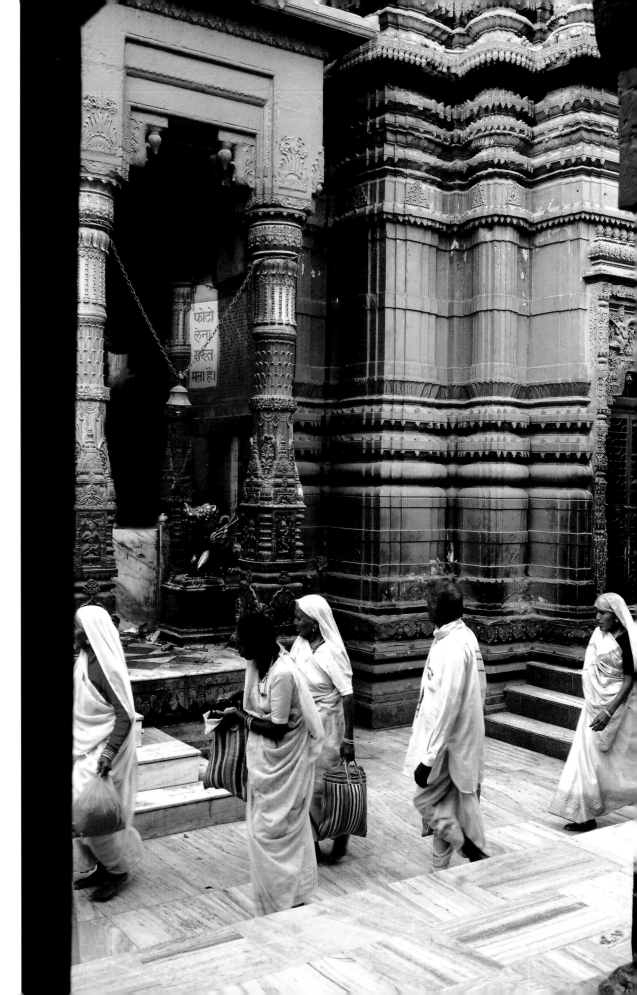

Preceding pages
The golden colours of the early hours of the morning. The faithful come down to the various ghats to make their ablutions before starting the day's work. The sexes are segregated by the use of different flights of steps, to protect their modesty. The women enter the water completely covered by their saris, and the men try not to look as the shapes of their bodies are revealed under clinging, wet clothing.

Opposite The temple of Durga, not far from the Assi ghat. Built in the eighteenth century in the style typical of northern India, the temple takes the form of a 'sikhara', consisting of five floors embellished with columns. Durga is the destructive incarnation of Parvati, Shiva's consort, who loves sacrifices. During the festivals dedicated to her, the heads of goats are sliced on the ritual altar.

Right One of the many erotic images carved in the teak beams of the Nepalese temple. They are part of a series of figures designed to teach the true way of Buddhism from birth to death. The message is simple: one must rise above earthly things and renounce the pleasures of life in order to attain enlightenment and be released from the cycle of reincarnation.

Opposite Ablutions on the ghat close to the majestic Alamgir mosque, constructed by the Moghul emperor Aurangzeb on the Panchganga ghat, previously the site of a large Hindu temple.

Right A shrine to the goddess Ganga faces the river. A priest pours a fresh oblation of sacred water, an act of paying homage and a sign of prayer.

Overleaf As dawn breaks, the moon sinks behind the cupolas of the Alamgir mosque.

Opposite Two brothers in a motorized rickshaw, one of the easiest ways to get around in the centre of Varanasi.

Right Signs and electric cables in the narrow streets of Varanasi.

Left A loom for weaving the silk for saris. In Varanasi this work is almost exclusively done by Muslim residents.

Opposite A picture of one of the narrow streets in the centre of Varanasi, close to the Chowk, the bustling civic heart of the city. Cows, which are sacred to the Hindus, are an immovable presence there, even amidst chaotic traffic.

A mass of souls seeking catharsis, each one turning to his own god before immersing himself in *maya*, in daily life; before commencing the struggle for survival, awaiting another night and the death that it may bring when Shiva chooses to show his destructive side.

The city revolves around itself. It is reflected in the river and refracts beauty back to itself. But the morning toilette only confirms my impression that the shades of night are only asleep, hidden away somewhere and ready to leap out again at any moment. On the left bank of the Ganges, the long row of palaces belonging to the maharaja and wealthy merchants resembles the stage set in a grand theatre. It is magnificent, sumptuous and solemn, and ostentatious in its splendour. Sultans dripping jewels strove to outdo each other here, resulting in tall cupolas of mosques that stand out unexpectedly, like boys who are too tall in the school photograph. All this to see on the left bank, but nothing at all on the right bank. Only emptiness, with the shores of the river stretching away for kilometres into infinity. Except in the monsoon season, when the river reclaims the space and regains ownership of it. The stage set has Varanasi as its backstage – a labyrinth of alleyways, steps, passageways and steep descents to the water's edge. The set is almost an escape from the masses, and from the stench in the air. Every gulley stinks, a receptacle for filth. (It is true that the youngsters collect the cow dung to dry it out for use as fuel for cooking. But who bothers about the rest of it? Seemingly no one.) In the maze of back-alleys behind the shops lurk the nocturnal spectres, the same ones that have been there for hundreds of years, only perhaps more numerous, multiplying with the passing of time. It is medieval and Indian. Medieval in a way that turns your stomach and does not let go, and is terribly real.

A bicycle-rickshaw driver queues up in the hope of some business from people coming back from the Dasaswamedh ghat. Next to him are the omnipresent cows.

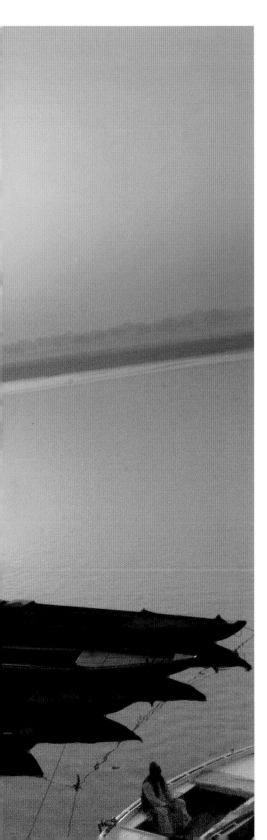

Opposite The sun rises over the Scindia ghat where the temple of Shiva is partially submerged in the waters of the Ganges. Built around one hundred and fifty years ago, it was so heavy that it sank into the water.

Right Ablutions under the umbrella near the Scindia ghat. Two men turn to face the rising sun, praying with clasped hands.

Preceding pages
The city's dirty laundry is washed in the waters of the Ganges by being pounded against stone slabs. This work is reserved for the lowest caste of untouchables.

Opposite Another typical morning scene on the ghats of Varanasi. Once washed in the river, the laundry is spread out to dry in the sunshine on the steps.

Right Morning ablutions are performed as the light of dawn suffuses the steps with a golden glow. The waters of the Ganges are all-cleansing, not only for washing dirty laundry, but also for washing away bad karma from the spirit.

Left and opposite
Ancient palaces flaunt
their decadent splendour
and display the riches
of their original owners.
These two are in the
centre, near the Chowk.
In the one on the left,
on the ground floor,
two statues of tigers are
still standing behind bars,
acting as guardians of
the entrance.

Overleaf The sun rises
over the deserted shores
of the river, which stretch
endlessly along the right
bank of the Ganges,
opposite Varanasi.
Especially on a Sunday,
the inhabitants of the city
cross over the river in search
of a place of tranquillity and
fewer crowds.

The Flat State
of Bihar

Preceding pages
Preceding pages
A group of young monks from Bhutan at morning prayer by the Maha Bodhi temple. As legend has it, it was on this very spot that Buddha attained enlightenment after forty-nine days of meditation.

Opposite Early morning at Patna, capital of the state of Bihar. Boats crowded with people arrive in the shallows of the great river. Here the water is cleaner, and there is less risk of contracting malaria during the ritual sacred bathing.

THE FERRY HAS JUST LEFT. From the riverbank we watch it puffing away across the Ganges, overloaded, like a steam train. The stretch of water before us looks more like a sea than a river. We can just make out the far banks, half-hidden by the humid heat-haze. Tonight there will be a full moon, and the families will make the most of it to celebrate a puja, an evening prayer, on the sandy riverbank. They will make offerings of flowers and rice to the river, and in return they will hope for good health and good fortune, if there is a god out there prepared to listen to their prayers.

A short distance away, they are pressing sugar cane to make molasses. This part of the Ganges is wedged like a blade between the fields of Bihar, its elevated banks slashed like wounds across the landscape. The river slices through the heart of India, dividing it into two pieces, north and south. There are no bridges here – there is no money with which to build them. Bihar is one of the poorest and most destitute states in the subcontinent, exhausted by the inactivity of governments devoted only to serving their own interests. These are malevolent riverbanks. Not only do they divide land, but also people. Over the last decade, a terrible caste war has broken out, costing the lives of over five thousand victims. Two sides are set against each other: the very poorest untouchables, known as Dalits, and the landlords, who therefore belong to the higher caste of Brahmins, Rajputs and Bhumihars. These are landowners who hold the destinies of millions of labourers in their hands, labourers sentenced to survive on a handful of rice grains. They fight with guns, and no shots are spared. Revenge is heaped upon revenge, and the slaughter continues as if in some Indian version of a Wild West movie. The dacoits, impromptu bands of brigands, attack villages and transportation because they are on fertile land. 'Strangers don't come here – even we ourselves are afraid of this India,' admitted one government official. He is a pea-brain, and arrogant to boot: 'Let me give you some advice: don't mix with the hoi-polloi. Trust me. Don't get out of your car, and take your photographs from out of the window. That's the best way.'

But these are a gentle people. Curious, and touchingly sweet-natured. Always ready with a smile. For them, a photograph is a present – for the group of children condemned to work in an open-air stone quarry, or forced to work in kilns, where clay sediment from the Ganges is used to make bricks. When the ferry arrives, the bank bustles with rickshaws, carts and vans. The dock is a heaving mass of merchandise and humanity; a jumble of fruit and vegetables. Sunburnt faces, and hands and feet painted with henna. I scan the eyes of those disembarking for traces of hatred, but all I see are the humble faces of dark-skinned labourers.

What is the human spirit concealing? How much suffering are we capable of inflicting? To think that it was actually here, in this fractured region of India, that the Buddha preached the truth, the way to be delivered from suffering. It was precisely at Bodh Gaya, a hundred or so kilometres south of the course of the Ganges, that he attained enlightenment, having meditated for forty-nine days, and overcome the trials set him by the demon Mara. A temple was built on this auspicious spot, and there is still a *ficus religiosa* (sacred fig tree) growing there, said to be a sapling of the original tree under which Prince Siddharta Gautama, later the Buddha, completed his ascetic journey and showed the way to Nirvana. Bihar literally means 'land of monasteries'. After the miraculous event, thousands of them sprang up all over the place – Hindu, Jain and, above all, Buddhist.

Patna, the city on the Ganges, and now capital of the state, seemed to have become the most important city in all India. Then called Pataliputra, it was the capital of the Maurya dynasty, whose principal ruler was King Aśoka, an enlightened monarch who in the third century BC brought the words of the Buddha to the whole of India. Today, the metropolis is a heaving mass of a million and a half residents, no less, where it is difficult to breathe. The traffic is so chaotic at rush hour that you run the risk of being trapped among the lorries for hours on end, breathing in the poisonous fumes. The English colonialists left their mark here in the form of an oversized warehouse like a giant beehive, known as Golghar. It is the only noteworthy thing about the city. It is a pity that it is abandoned, as well as ugly. The Buddha had predicted all this: 'This will be a land of war, fire and floods,' he prophesied. He came to show the true way to escape from all this suffering. But it is uncertain whether his word succeeded in reaching humanity.

I wake up in the city of Munger, on the right bank of the Ganges. The first golden rays of the rising sun light up the streets, still deserted apart from the motorized rickshaws. Soon there will be chaos, and the traffic will dominate the streets as the electric wires have dominated the skyline.

Opposite The coloured powder used to adorn the face and head during religious rites.

Right A young woman who has arrived in Patna from the countryside. She is squatting on the steps of the Mahendra ghat. She is accompanied by her husband and little boy. The journey is a unique cause for celebration, as the child will be taking his first ceremonial bath in the waters of the Ganges, and later the family will go to the nearby market to make some purchases.

Overleaf A sandy island created when the water level of the Ganges is low. During the monsoon season, the waters rise and these surfaces are submerged. In the meantime, they provide a place of refuge from the crowds and a source of cleaner water for those who want to make their ablutions and pray.

Opposite Yoga practice on a small sand island formed by the Ganges near Patna. The *yogin* has just collected some of the river water in the receptacle by his side.

Right A woman pours water from the Ganges on to an altar in the form of the lingam and the *yoni*, emblems of Shiva. The liquid runs along a purification channel after being in contact with the deity. The lingam represents the phallus, and the yoni represents the vulva; their union symbolizes the union of the earth and sky, the oneness of existence. As well as being the god of ascetics and self-denial, Shiva is principally worshipped as a sexual deity, sex being an intrinsic part of all things.

Opposite The banks of the Ganges near Rajmahal, with the silhouette of a rook in the foreground.

Right A woman at prayer in a shrine facing the Ganges near Rajmahal, a small town of ancient origin that still retains important relics of its Islamic past.

Overleaf Sunset over the Ganges, not far from Munger. The silhouettes of the trees trace a delicate pattern across the fiery sky. As it crosses the state of Bihar, the river provides us with unexpected glimpses of nature. At times as wide as the sea; at times dividing into smaller rivulets, which saturate the small villages dependent on agriculture for their livelihood. It is a picture of an India relatively untouched by the process of modernization and the developments of recent years.

Left and opposite
Work at a kiln, which produces bricks using clay earth from sediments found along the Ganges. The oxen are used to work a rudimentary mechanism for mixing the basis. The bricks are then moulded and brought to the kiln to be fired. The work is not just done by men, but also by women and children. Young boys and girls work from dawn till dusk for a handful of rupees.

Overleaf A group of boats moored along the banks of the Ganges.

Tens, hundreds, thousands of prostrations are made daily. It is exhausting physical exercise, although they seem engrossed, even relaxed as they walk in a clockwise direction round the Maha Bodhi temple. Some of them are monks, but there are also ordinary people, Nepalese, Bhutanese, peasants from the Himalayas. Some of the women are wearing the traditional Tibetan skirt with a horizontally striped apron. Others are simply walking along, fingering their rosary beads. Some are chanting a prayer, a chant that is echoed a thousand times and rises to the sky above. If it is possible for the spirit to resonate, then it would be in this place on the Ganges that it would be most likely to happen. This is Bodh Gaya, one of the four most important sites of Buddhist pilgrimage. Here the Buddha came to the enlightened recognition that it is desire that chains humanity to the infinite cycle of birth and death.

My bare feet pad down the steps and lead me down to the bottom. One single step inside the temple and all is an oasis of calm. For the moment, India is outside the gates. There are no pictures of horrifying gods or their zoomorphic faces. There is only a solemn, gilded image of the Enlightened One. My glance falls on the muddy shoes of an old lady struggling to genuflect. Her hands are calloused, and her clothes threadbare. Who knows what sacrifices she has made to get here, what mountain she has left behind her? Her husband helps her, his dark leather jacket worn out by years of wear and tear. He also has the ruddy face of one accustomed to excessive amounts of exhausting work. What desires would these two old people have had? From which of them would they need to be freed in order to escape the cycle of samsara?

Lights fuelled by butter burning in front of the images of the Buddha found on the outer wall of the Maha Bodhi temple, built on the spot where Siddharta Gautama, the future prophet, sat under a peepul, or fig tree, before attaining enlightenment.

Left An ancient statue of Buddha.

Opposite Worship held under the fig tree that is said to have come from an offshoot of the original tree, which grew here two thousand five hundred years ago. To commemorate this great event, two hundred and fifty years after the Buddha reached enlightenment, King Aśoka built a convent and a *vajrasana*, a throne of diamonds. Bodh Gaya is one of the four most sacred places in Buddhism, and therefore a destination for pilgrimages. Particularly in winter, it attracts the devout from all over India and the Himalayan regions, who often undertake long and arduous journeys to get there.

Overleaf A Buddhist monk performs an infinite number of prostrations, walking clockwise around the Maha Bodhi temple. It is a laborious task, but this act of humility leads to purification, which can overcome the suffering involved in the samsara, the cycle of reincarnation.

Opposite Night falls over the Maha Bodhi temple. The religious ceremonies are nearly over. They start well before dawn. A magnetic silence envelops the visitors and the devout, who are continuing the ritual walk. A yellow light emanates from the large figure of the Buddha on the main altar; his solemn face seems to change aspect through the different times of day.

Right Monks continue their own prayers: here rosary beads and grains of rice are sprinkled in a cascade over the surface of a smooth copper dish. The gesture is repeated an infinite number of times. It is the offering of the *mandala*, asking for blessing to continue the spiritual journey.

Overleaf Two monks from the Himalayan regions consult a liturgical text during a religious celebration.

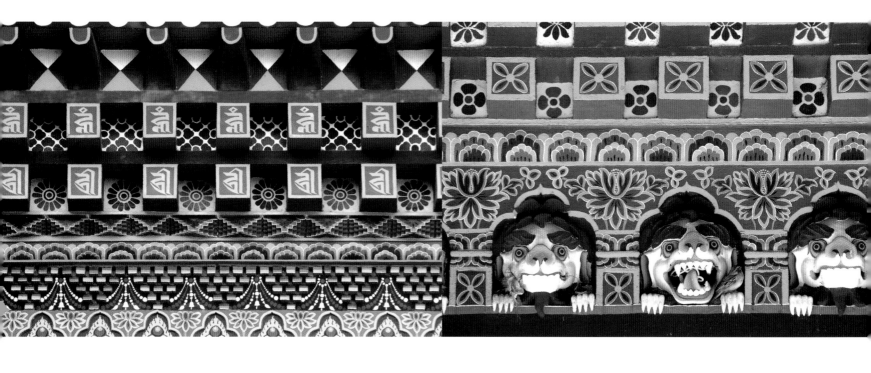

Opposite For centuries a sleepy place, today Bodh Gaya is undergoing a rapid re-awakening. The Indian government receives a wealth of income from the devout who go there on pilgrimage. Nearly all the states where Buddhism is the prevalent religion have constructed temples according to their own architectural styles. On the left are two decorative features from the Bhutan temple.

Right A Buddhist monk circling the Maha Bodhi temple in prayer. He is spinning a prayer wheel, or *mani khorlo*, and repeating incessantly the mantra 'om ma ni pad me hung', which is said to purify man from earthly suffering.

Preceding pages
An enormous banyan
tree shades the banks
of the Ganges on a sunny
summer's afternoon in the
region around Bhagalpur.

Left An evening bath for
buffalo in a swampy area
close to the course of
the Ganges.

Opposite A pilgrim on
the banks of the Ganges
carrying provisions for his
spiritual journey, a journey
that will lead him to the
temple of Ajgaivinath,
also known as Gaibinath
Mahadeo, situated close
to Sultanganj. Dedicated to
Shiva, the temple is one of
the most important places
of pilgrimage for Hindus in
this part of India. According
to legend, this was the
home of the sage Jahnu,
whose meditations were
interrupted by the roar of
the Ganges rushing from
the Himalayas towards
the ocean. Angry at being
disturbed, the sage
swallowed up the river
completely. It took the
intervention of King
Bhagiratha to help him to
see reason: he decided to
release the river by making
an incision in his thigh
through which it could
flow out again.

Opposite and right
In the dry season, massive ancient carvings are visible around the base of the granite block upon which the temple of Ajgaivinath was built. The origins of the temple are unknown. It is known that it was not destroyed by the Islamic sultans, unlike the temple of Parvati, which once towered over a nearby promontory on the left bank of the Ganges, but was replaced by a mosque (opposite). In this whole area, archaeologists have made important discoveries of relics belonging to kingdoms just before and after the beginning of the Christian era. The Maurya made Patna their capital and dominated the whole of southern India. Then came the Sunga and the Gupta dynasties, who held power until the beginning of the seventh century. The reign of the last kingdom was a golden age for the arts and for religion, especially Buddhism. During construction work on the new railway, a magnificent statue of the Buddha, two and a half metres in height, was found in the mud at Sultanganj.

Overleaf The Ganges, divided into several branches near Bhagalpur, can be crossed with greater ease by peasants cultivating the fertile land on the islands created by the force of the current.

he Ganges
oghly?

THE BUFFALO ARE IN THE WATER, SWIMMING AROUND. They have been pulling ploughs all day long in the rice fields, and now they are enjoying a restorative bath. A boy is minding them from the bank, wielding a bamboo branch. Soon he will take them back to their stalls. Not far away a few caulkers are building a boat. They are using a bow drill to make holes to accommodate wooden rivets. The smell of pitch assails the nostrils. Rajmahal is a small, sleepy town. A few mosques hark back to its distant Islamic origins. We go down to the riverbank. Here the Ganges has reached the region of Bengal, which is now divided into two due to the schism that has affected India. West Bengal remains within the borders of India, while East Bengal is part of Bangladesh. A fragmented territory, torn apart by man trying to establish a line of demarcation between the different religious faiths: Hindus here, Muslims over there. As if a line drawn on a map could decide which god was worshipped where. The separation of religions causes intolerance, and, in the case of a mixed marriage, leads to violence.

Religious conflict has deep roots in India. Islam arrived on the shores of the subcontinent a thousand years ago; Mohammed brought Arabic culture and that of central Asia with him. Today, despite the creation of two Islamic states, Pakistan and Bangladesh, a huge number of people in India still believe in the *Koran*, perhaps as many as a hundred million. This figure makes India the fourth largest Islamic state in the world. A great proportion of these people are concentrated along the borders. In West Bengal the minarets follow one another in quick succession, like flags hoisted to mark the religious allegiance of the villages. It is here that the Ganges senses the call of the ocean. It inclines once again to the south-east, and starts to divide. The larger branch flows into Bangladesh and merges with the Brahmaputra; the other heads decisively south shortly before the border. This is the Bhagirathi, which the English colonialists nicknamed the Hooghly, and it is this river that the Indians believe to be the true course of the Ganges, the sacred course. It is no coincidence that it has been named after the mythical king. Consequently, the mouth of the Bhagirathi is thought to be that of the great river.

The first city along the way is Malda. Today is a festival day, and people are washing themselves outdoors in the public fountains; there are small groups carrying soap, towels and toothpaste. There is water everywhere, invading the streets. Rickshaws are darting here and there, laden with people. Coloured saris are billowing in the wind. In colonial times, Malda was christened Bazaar by the English, and it was a key junction for commercial traffic. In those days, the Bhagirathi was an important means of transportation to the Bay of Bengal, where the East India Company had built a new port close to a small village at the mouth of the delta. Later on, the port took the name of Calcutta, and subsequently became a megalopolis of fifteen million inhabitants. But back in the eighteenth century, Bengal was a strong and independent state, ruled by a nawab who considered himself the last descendant of a long dynasty. Indeed, from the twelfth century onwards, the banks of the Bhagirathi and its tributaries witnessed the flourishing of several Islamic kingdoms, which succeeded those kingdoms belonging to the Buddhist and Hindu faiths. Over several centuries of different Islamic influences, the one that seems most significant was the sultanate that became established at Gaur, which is located close to Bangladesh. The village is now a collection of magnificent ruins. Fortifications, mosques and minarets paint a picture of a sumptuous and glorious India. Decor, tiles, mosaics and inlay-work survive as relics of a past that sprouted up among the paddy-fields. The Qadam Rasul mosque is still a place of pilgrimage for Muslims today, for the mosque contains a precious relic in the form of a footprint made by Mohammed.

Islam flourished in Bengal after 1707, when the entire region became an independent state, governed by its own nawab. The old kingdom has long since disappeared, but the ancient capital of Murshidabad is determined not to let its brilliance be completely dimmed by the passing years. It is dusk when we arrive, and already the courting couples have taken their places to watch the red sunset over the river, next to the mosque. A few cows are grazing on the meadow opposite. Horse-drawn carts are to-ing and fro-ing frantically beneath the entrance archway to the city.

With each new step we take, a forgotten India is slowly uncovered. Ancient palaces conjure up pictures from dog-eared history books, and glory and ambition lie buried within their walls.

Opposite The high banks of the Ganges carved out in the clayey ground near Malda. Note the lack of dykes. During the monsoon season, the river breaks its banks, and the fields are flooded with an abundance of water.

Right A woman working in the fields: after harvesting, the rice is left to dry in the sun, and then poured down from above, making use of the gusts of wind to help sort the grains from the chaff.

Overleaf A peasant straddling a buffalo in a flooded paddy-field near the small town of Malda. In Bengal, the water levels rise alarmingly during the wet season, and vast areas become flooded. As a result, it is extremely difficult to get around.

Opposite A farmer waiting to board a boat at Manikchwak, a small river port on the Ganges, an hour's drive from Malda.

Right Unloading fruit and vegetables to be taken to market. Farmers and merchants take their goods to different places on the river. The Ganges may divide, but it is still an important communications link, and very useful for the transportation of goods. In this part of India, there are few roads, and those that do exist are in very poor condition. Enormous potholes, stretches without tarmac and frequent deviations conspire to make every journey an ordeal. Travelling by car, you need to reckon on a maximum speed of 30 kilometres an hour on major roads, which is reduced to 20 kilometres on minor ones.

Left Details of enamelled bricks adorning the façade of the Gumti gateway, which was probably the entrance to the prisons inside the fortified citadel of Gaur. The structure, which is surmounted by a circular cupola, was built in 1512. Gaur was an ancient and powerful Islamic city. Today, it is a drowsy agricultural village north of Malda, not far from the border with Bangladesh.

Opposite The Gumti gateway. The monuments of Gaur, the mosques and the ancient walls of the royal palace are destinations for groups of Indians and school parties. They remain important relics from the first Islamic sultanates in Bengal.

Overleaf The imposing Dakhil Darwaza gateway.

Opposite A group of young women return home to their village by horse-drawn cart, having visited the sights of Gaur.

Right Rickshaws are a frequent means of transport in rural areas. Their owners are very proud of them, and love to embellish them with designs, and paint them in loud colours.

Overleaf Lukochuri Darwaza, the gateway through which the sultans entered the citadel of Gaur.

Preceding pages
Sunset over the cupolas and minarets of the Chandeni mosque in the heart of the beautiful city of Murshidabad, another important Islamic city, rich in history. Stretching along the Bhagirathi, it was once the ancient capital of the Islamic region of Bengal, founded by the emperor Akbar. Between 1704 and 1790 it was the residence of the nawab, the sultan.

Left A moment of collective prayer in front of a mosque on an important day in the Islamic calendar, Eid Al-Adha, commemorating Abraham's sacrifice of a goat, after God had tested his faith by asking him to sacrifice his own son Isaac. In cities and villages, Indians who are believers in the *Koran* hold celebrations and literally throng the streets on their way to pray. At this time of year, some of them also set off on the *hajj*, the pilgrimage to Mecca.

Opposite One of the noble palaces in Murshidabad, which, although threatened by decay and neglect, proudly resists the march of time.

Left Paper for recycling is weighed in a village shop near Krishnanagar.

Opposite A woman from Berhampore spinning with traditional instruments on the street. This small town on the banks of the Bhagirathi is an important centre of silk production. The thread is used to weave valuable sari material, which is prized by Indian women.

Wars and intrigues reveal themselves as we make our way towards the magnificent Hazarduari, the palace of a thousand gates, and seat of the sovereign. In 1756 the ambitious nawab Siraj-ud-daula wrested the spreading town of Calcutta from the hands of the English. However, it was unfortunate that the following year he was betrayed by his uncle, who was the military commander-in-chief, at the strategic battle of Plassey, an event that opened the door to the colonization of Bengal. The uncle was rewarded with a puppet-throne in return.

Before flowing into the sea, the Hooghly, or Ganges, waters Calcutta. The city is mad and chaotic, full of appalling tragedy and poverty. It is a synthesis of all the contradictions that constitute India; as a capital city it was once even grandiose. (Under the English it was the seat of the Viceroy of British India until 1911, when there were strong bids for independence within the city.) But it can also be a tranquil place, bound up in the concentrated observance of collective rites and Hindu ceremonies. A visit to the temple of the goddess Kali confirms the strong pulse of ancient blood coursing through people's veins: the traditional cycle continues as the temple priests decapitate goats to propitiate the goddess, slicing their heads with a terrifying axe. Blood is spurting everywhere, and shivers go up and down the spines of those watching. Mother Teresa set to work here, helping the dispossessed of the city, those escaping from the countryside, Hindu refugees from Islamic Bangladesh, and orphans. The border with Bangladesh has created a historical caesura.

This afternoon we have come down to the ghat called Eden Garden. There is a large crowd of people making their way down to the Hooghly. The majestic Howrah Bridge rises up above our heads. It is a single arc 450 metres long – like the flight of a bird winging its way between shores. It is spectacular from here, but absolute hell on the bridge itself: it is the most crowded bridge in the world, and at rush hour you can be stuck in a traffic jam indefinitely. It is an image that suits Calcutta – the city is like a bird flying over a sacred river.

An image symbolizing Calcutta, the capital of Bengal. The grandiose bridge named Vidyasagar Setu, 457 metres long, spans the Hooghly river (the Ganges to the Indians).

Preceding pages
A long line of the devout, queuing early to get into the inner sanctuary of the temple at Dakshineswar, on the right bank of the Hooghly, north of Calcutta. The temple is dedicated to the goddess Kali.

Left A religious festival in honour of Sarasvati, consort of Brahma, goddess of knowledge and the arts. A devotee lifts up a statue representing the goddess, and is about to throw it into the sacred waters of the Ganges as a sign of homage. This rite takes place in January, and is typical of the rites celebrated in Bengal.

Opposite An improvised altar at the foot of a peepul tree, or *ficus religiosa*, on the banks of the Ganges near Calcutta. The elephant-headed god Ganesha, son of Shiva, bringer of good fortune and success, is visible on the left. He is considered to be benevolent, and a remover of obstacles.

Preceding pages
Two Sikhs walking by the small lake in the Victoria Memorial Park, which forms part of a vast green area in the city, known as the Maidan.

Opposite A rickshaw pulled by hand. This has always been a traditional mode of transport in India, but today it has been almost totally superseded by the bicycle or motorized versions.

Below An image of abject poverty in Calcutta. These street camps are the dwelling-places of thousands of homeless people.

Left Palm-reading amid the chaos on the Nimtolla ghat, where cremations take place.

Opposite Another scene on the Nimtolla ghat. Children decorate their hands with stamps that look like henna designs.

Overleaf A group of boys in festive mood returning by truck from the religious festival on the Babu ghat. The festival is in honour of Durga, the malign incarnation of Parvati, consort of Shiva, who has the power to kill demons.

The Thousand–fingered Delta

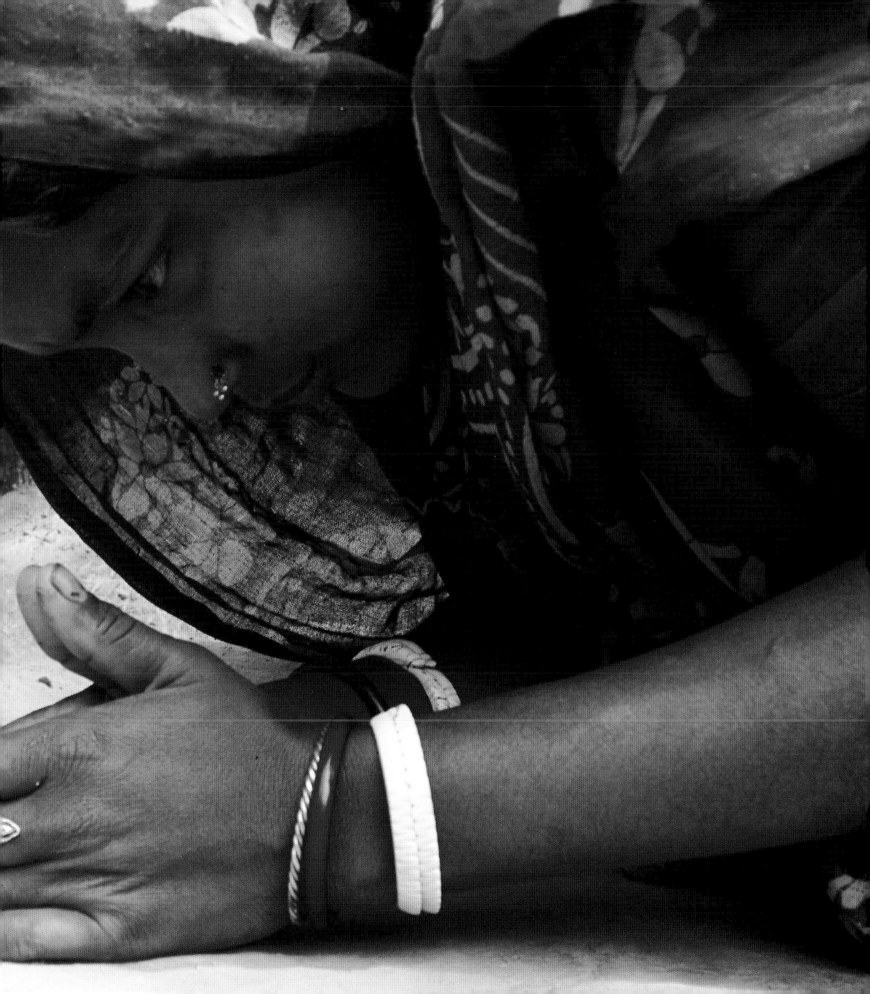

'WE ALWAYS LIVE IN FEAR OF BEING DEVOURED.' Rahal, a seventeen-year-old, has dark skin and ivory teeth. In her green sari, she looks like a princess or a goddess who has appeared here among the paddy-fields. They are still dry, waiting for the rainy season, a flat expanse criss-crossed with irrigation channels. At the bottom of the fields, beyond the bank, the Ganges flows past solemnly. Rahal shies away from me; she is embarrassed to talk. She is not used to meeting white-skinned foreigners. She is on her way to school with two friends – it is a walk that takes three-quarters of an hour. There is no transport on the small island, which is a part of the archipelago comprising the Ganges Delta. Everybody walks everywhere, even the teachers. The elementary-school teacher arrives, and he too looks about him cautiously. 'Every year ten or so people get eaten by the tigers; people fishing or working in the fields. You can never relax. But we have become used to it. It is our destiny. It would be unthinkable to move away from here. We would only join the long line of unemployed in Calcutta.' The teacher's tone conveys some bitterness, and he hurries on. He is late; school begins at eleven and the pupils will be waiting for him. He will take the register, hoping that everyone will be present, hoping that no tigers will be present.

Similar stories are to be heard all over the islands that constitute the Sundarbans. This is a protected area. Unesco has designated 2,585 square kilometres of the Ganges Delta as a World Heritage Site, for the simple reason that two hundred and fifty Bengal tigers live here, a species threatened with extinction, which has been placed under protection by India and neighbouring

Bangladesh. The tigers will be protected, but what about the people? It is not easy to live with a big cat on your doorstep. Therefore life has become cheap – worth a few hundred euros in fact, the amount of money paid by the West Bengal government as compensation to those families who have lost someone through an attack by a tiger. The stories are dramatic: fishermen devoured in their boats, farmers attacked in the fields, doors and windows torn open by tigers that are too old to hunt and so have become man-eaters. Added to this there are the disastrous cyclones, which rage furiously along the coast of Bengal, and then the floods that cause rivers to burst their banks, homes to be smashed to pieces and harvests ruined. Here, at the end of the sacred river, life is an endless cycle of suffering, and God seems absent.

From Calcutta, it takes a whole day to reach the Sundarbans. The first stage is done by road, then by ferry, then by bicycle-rickshaw across an island, then finally by boat again. There is something unreal about the whole journey, as if it has come out of another era. In the course of a day, the jumbled chaos of Calcutta has been left behind, and replaced by the silence of the canals in the Delta, interrupted only by the lapping of the water, voices lost in the mangrove swamps, the sound of bicycle wheels, the only means of transport on the islands, and the swishing of fishermen's nets being cast into the water. When we finally arrive, it is evening. Night has fallen suddenly, plunging everything into utter darkness. There are no street lights. Now there are different sounds emerging: bells ringing in the village's small Hindu temple. The puja, the evening prayer, is being presided over by a bare-chested priest. The rays of an oil-lamp illuminate the divinities of the delta. Firstly there is Dakshinaroy, the monstrous tiger-headed creature, then Shiber Kumir, the crocodile infesting the canals, then Ma Bonobibi, the goddess of the forest. At first light, before the working day begins, small sacred fires are lit along the banks of the Ganges. Offerings of flowers and bowls of rice are floated on the water. Then everything continues as normal: women filling up buckets at the well, children looking after the animals, the goats and oxen. Men fishing in boats, or chopping wood, cutting down trees in the impenetrable mangrove forest. The logs are transported into town, where they are sold as fuel for the huge funeral pyres that are used to cremate the dead, as is required by Hindu tradition, in honour of the goddess Ganga.

Today, our entire time has been spent haggling and trying to find information. It would appear to be some kind of mission impossible to find a boat that will take us from the heart of the Sundarbans, across the maze of waterways, and as far as Ganga Sagar, the mystical island. The name of this outermost piece of land means 'river-sea'. The name says it all: this island is the point at which the sacred river merges with the ocean. For Hindus, this land is sacred. Dozens of shrines and dharmashalas are clustered on the shores, gazing into the infinite space beyond.

A group of girls in uniform return home from school on the island of Ganga Sagar, the last island in the Ganges Delta before the Indian Ocean begins.

Opposite An altar erected between the waterways of the Ganges Delta in the heart of the Sundarbans, a protected area due to the endangered Bengal tigers. This powerful feline poses a real threat to the inhabitants, and features prominently in their popular iconography, perhaps to ward them off. Altars are often built in much-frequented areas such as riverbanks, village streets and mooring stations for the boats. There is danger lurking not only in the form of the tigers, who claim dozens of victims each year, but also from poisonous snake-bites and crocodile attacks.

Below A group of men on their way to cut down trees in the mangrove forest of the Sundarbans. When woodcutters, fishermen or farmers leave the village, they always wear a mask depicting a human face on the back of their heads, in the hope that the tigers will not attack them. It is thought that they only attack from behind and that if the tiger thinks that it has been discovered, it will give up and run away.

Overleaf A fisherman casting his net into a pond in the delta.

Left Bicycles are virtually the only form of transport on the islands of the delta. Very few of them have roads suitable for motor vehicles.

Opposite A young woman waters the plants in her field from a water-jar. Most of the agricultural work is done by hand.

Overleaf People at work in the fields just after sunrise.

Left A woman wearing a green sari returns home, carrying a jar full of water. The women's deportment makes them look more like graceful princesses than country folk.

Opposite A group of women waiting their turn at the spring. Water is a very precious commodity in the Ganges Delta. Morning and evening, the women have the task of fetching water from the spring to use at home.

Overleaf Using a wooden tool, an old woman rakes over the grains of rice spread out to dry in the yard outside her house.

Opposite A rudimentary system of transferring water from one canal to another in order to irrigate the crops in the fields.

Right Rich spoils for the fisherman – a good catch of scampi, which he is taking to market.

Left A boy washes himself with river water after a long day's work as a cabin boy on a ferry.

Opposite A sadhu travels between the islands of the delta by boat. To pass the time, he intones religious songs and provides a rhythmic accompaniment for himself using a pair of small metal cymbals.

Overleaf Fishermen on the Hooghly, or Ganges, near Diamond Harbour. This location is already regarded as the mouth of the river, as the estuary is very wide, and before long the freshwater will merge with the saltwater of the sea.

Every year, during the full moon in January, tens of thousands of pilgrims converge here to pray to *Ganga Ma*. Even if it is hard to think of this as the true finishing point of the grand and sacred river, legend proves to be stronger than fact.

Ganga Sagar is the final destination on our journey. According to the Indians, this island at the mouth of the Hooghly is the last fragment of land to be lapped by the waters of the sacred river. So this is the last trace of the Ganges? After travelling so many miles from the source to the delta, it is slightly disappointing. Is this it? A beach and the sea stretching away into the distance. Shekar, our Bengali friend, is more convinced. Why else would this temple, dedicated to the goddess Ganga, have been built here? Why else would there be so many sadhus living here in makeshift huts? So many people in prayer? Why indeed? Maybe because myth needs to have some concrete reference points; maybe it needs to dwell in places that are named on a map, places where people can go to pray. Our footprints disappear in the sand, as nebulous as the differing responses of faith.

Here the river flows in a long curve, creating an area of shallows where a few fishing boats are anchored. They look like the old Arab dhows, with tall, slender prows. The foreshore has been smoothed over by the undertow. A young woman dressed in red is raking the wet sand, looking for coins thrown into this far-flung stretch of river by pilgrims. She admits that she would rather do this than go begging. 'What I receive is then due to my own efforts,' she says earnestly. Meanwhile, the sun sinks deeper towards the horizon. A group of older women approach. They hurry down to the river to pray. They remove their shoes and dip their feet in the water. Then they turn to face the sunset, hands clasped together. One of them intones a votive song, and the others join in. They lift their hands to the sky. Then they look curiously at me. One of them comes up to me and asks: 'What are you doing here? Why are you not praying?'

Left A monkey sitting on the branch of a tree near a wharf in the Sundarbans National Park.

Opposite A sadhu with a budgerigar perched on his shoulder at the Kapila Muni temple on the island of Ganga Sagar, the last place of worship along the Ganges before it meets the ocean. The island is a destination for pilgrims all year round. In the middle of January, there is an important religious festival that draws crowds from all over India.

Left A priest raises his palm to bless the faithful in one of the temples on the delta.

Opposite Yet more hands – these ones belong to a craftsman who sculpts figures of gods and goddesses out of clay.

Overleaf Precarious wooden bridges traverse the waterways, criss-crossing the island of Ganga Sagar.

Left An old peasant woman with strikingly proud and noble features, pictured outside her mud hut on the island of Ganga Sagar.

Opposite A woman lighting the fire in a clay oven in order to cook the evening meal, which will consist of dal, a mixture of rice and soup. Some days, if they are lucky, there may also be some fish.

Opposite A girl leaving her home by means of a bridge – a single tree trunk spanning one of the waterways in the delta.

Right A village in the Ganges Delta. It is common practice for villagers to dig a lake so that they can farm their own fish. Otherwise they will wait to profit from the flooding during the monsoon season, when fish are easier to catch as they are forced out of the canals and into swampy areas.

Overleaf The sun sets over the beach on the island of Ganga Sagar, lapped by the waves of the Indian Ocean. Wooden fishing boats are at anchor, waiting to brave the waves again the following day at the crack of dawn.

Opposite An evening ceremony in the Kapila Muni temple on the island of Ganga Sagar. Kapila Muni is a sage who appears in the legend of the birth of the Ganges. He is said to have burnt King Sagara's sixty thousand children to ashes, because they disturbed him while he was meditating.

Right A woman offers flowers to a statue of the goddess Ganga inside the temple.

Left A rudimentary table for offerings at the foot of the sacred peepul tree. Creativity flourishes with the most basic of means: a splash of colour, some stones, a few garlands. The trident fork shows that this offering is a tribute to the god Shiva.

Opposite A long-haired sadhu outside his shabby hut on the beach, at the point where the Hooghly-Ganges discharges its waters into the sea.

As the sun sets over the sea, it is time for evening prayer. This is the end of the Ganges, but its waters surge onwards unceasingly, merging with the ocean in an endless flow of being, to which man has given the name Life.

Translated from the Italian by Clare Costa

First published in the United Kingdom in 2005 by
Thames & Hudson Ltd, 181A High Holborn, London WC1V 7QX

www.thamesandhudson.com

First published in 2005 in hardcover in the United States of America by
Thames & Hudson Inc., 500 Fifth Avenue, New York, New York 10110

thamesandhudsonusa.com

Original edition © 2005 Magnus Edizioni SpA, Udine
This edition © 2005 Thames & Hudson Ltd, London

British Library Cataloguing-in-Publication Data
A catalogue record for this book is available from the British Library

ISBN-13: 978-0-500-51259-3
ISBN-10: 0-500-51259-0

Library of Congress Catalog Number
2005923453

Printed in Italy by Litoimmagine Rodeano Alto UD, Italy